D0557768

You Can
Get
Published

PEGGY TEETERS

WRITER'S DIGEST BOOKS
CINCINNATI, OHIO

Other fine Writer's Digest Books are available from your local bookstore or direct from the publisher.

02 01 00 99 98   5 4 3 2 1

Library of Congress Cataloging-in-Publication Data

Teeters, Peggy
    You can get published / by Peggy Teeters; [content edited by Roseann S. Biederman].—
1st ed.
        p.   cm.
    Includes index.
    ISBN 0-89879-828-0 (alk. paper)
    1. Authorship. I. Biederman, Roseann S. II. Title.
PN151.T44   1998
808'.02—dc21   97-47539
                                                                                              CIP

Edited by Roseann Biederman
Production edited by Patrick Souhan
Cover design by Brian Roeth
Interior design by Sandy Kent

About the Author

Peggy Teeters, a former army wife, has traveled to many countries and has lived in Germany and Japan. She has used these backgrounds for her articles, children's stories, columns, books and TV scripts. She is a teacher as well as a writer, with a B.S. degree from St. Norbert College in Wisconsin. She has taught for twenty years in the Arlington Adult Education Program, and has taught creative writing at the University of Virginia for seven years. She is a member of the Society of Children's Book Writers and Mystery Writers of America. She was listed in *Who's Who of American Women for 1970* and *Who's Who in America for 1994*. She is the mother of four sons and one daughter.

Walker Publishers recently published Teeters's biography on Jules Verne for young adults, and Cloverdale came out with a novel for teenage girls, *Weekend Romance*, featuring West Point.

She is currently working on a novel for the ten-to-fourteen age group called *Get Ready Here Comes the 21st Century*, and has begun her first mystery for adults, *Marked for Murder*.

Acknowledgments

I'd like to thank all of the people in my writing classes for their input, and give a special thanks to Cindy Hohner, who helped to make my manuscript look professional.

TABLE OF CONTENTS

1 DON'T WAIT TO COMMUNICATE

Get ready to enter the world of Shakespeare, Shelley, Byron, Keats, Milton, Dante, Dickens, Stevenson, Eliot, the Brownings, Dickinson, Frost and the many other writers of the past. These men and women left a legacy for mankind to cherish and enjoy. But the writers of today are also contributing to that special gift, and it isn't too late for you to join them. Decide right now to learn how to become a writer and use your creative powers. There's no doubt about it—you can do it!

If it's been years since you read the works of the literary giants, browse at your library and again become immersed in genius. But as you reread *Hamlet* or "Ode to the West Wind," go one step further. Do some research on the lives of these writers and jot down some of the details. You'll find that these people experienced the problems we all encounter in our daily lives. Eventually, your notes will add up to a feature article, or at least some interesting fillers that point out some of these great writers' human frailties.

For example, you'll discover that John Keats knew only too well that feeling of life slipping by too quickly. All of us, whether we are twenty or sixty, experience that sensation now and then, and wish we could stop the hands of time. Keats, especially, was overwhelmed by the thought that he could never finish what he had set out to accomplish. One of his poems begins

When I have fears that I may cease to be
Before my pen has gleaned my teeming brain . . .

It's possible that he had a premonition about an early death; he was only twenty-five when he died from tuberculosis. But in that short time, he managed to write some of the purest poetry in any literature and carved a niche for himself in the field of English Romanticism. And who can't help but be inspired by this line from one of his poems: "A thing of beauty is a joy forever"?

As you rub elbows—if only briefly—with writers of the past and present, ask yourself what characteristics apply to all of them. You'll soon come to the conclusion that communicativeness heads the list: They all had the desire to share their innermost thoughts and feelings with the world. Isn't this your dream too? Here, then, is your link to those creative men and women you so much admire. But writers of all ages are also versatile, moody, absentminded, sensitive, individualistic, persevering, determined and enthusiastic. Add a sense of humor to that list of adjectives, and you'll have the definition of someone who is a professional writer—or destined to be. If you take a good, honest look at yourself and you fit this description, you're on your way to qualifying for the job of wordsmith.

Are you worried because you know that you can only write on a part-time basis? Chase all your fears away. William Faulkner wrote his novel, *As I Lay Dying*, in six weeks. Phillis Wheatley worked on her book of poetry whenever her duties as a slave allowed her a moment or two. Jane Austen scribbled notes for her novels in the midst of family conversations. Maya Angelou dredged up memories of her childhood while she danced, sang and traveled, and finally produced a remarkable autobiography, *I Know Why the Caged Bird Sings*. Frances Trollope started her writing career at fifty—and turned out 115 books, mainly novels and accounts of her travels.

Creativity seems to flourish at any age, with the proper nourishment. During the past five years, teachers in elementary and junior high schools have experimented with creative writing workshops held after class, and have been amazed at the response and the results. They found that students were able to sell poems, articles and stories to well-known juvenile magazines. What also surprised teachers was that more than twenty editors are looking for young writers to send in material and receive their first byline; some of these magazines also pay their contributors.

Several publications now run writing contests for young adults. The winners not only get their names in print, but also receive a tidy sum of money. What is even more newsworthy is the sudden interest in fiction. Beginning writers now have the chance to become the storytellers they've always wanted to be. This is the time to learn how to do it.

But do the creative juices still flow when an individual reaches the "golden years"? According to the experts, creativity never dries up, and more importantly, the creative process can actually add years to your life. It brings out positive and constructive attitudes in you, and results in remarkable works of art or handicrafts or literature. Many older men and women have won acclaim: Pablo Casals played the cello and conducted orchestras up until the time of his death at ninety-six; Grandma Moses took up painting at the age of seventy-seven; Carl Sandburg wrote his six-volume biography of Lincoln when he was in his sixties and seventies; and Agatha Christie came up with another whodunit when she was eighty.

And what about the unknowns? Do they stand a chance against the established writers? They certainly do. Dr. James Herriot didn't dream that his homespun stories about his experiences as a veterinarian in Yorkshire, England, would win him fame and fortune. Stephen King didn't know, when he quit his job as an English teacher to devote all of his time to writing, that his horror novels would meet with great success. Maxine Hong Kingston was more than surprised when her memoirs, *The Woman Warrior*, received high praise from the American, as well as the Chinese, community. Mary Ellen Pinkham didn't have an inkling that her collection of household hints would become a top-ten best-seller. Richard Nelson

3

Boles didn't expect to see his book *What Color Is Your Parachute?* become a guide in many career courses. In 1992, another unknown named Robert James Waller wrote *The Bridges of Madison County* and became famous. Despite dismal reviews, the book managed to make *The New York Times* best-seller list.

Robert Fontaine, a humorist who has written hundreds of light-hearted pieces for the *Saturday Evening Post* and other periodicals, wrote the following words for the beginning writer in *The Writer's Handbook*:

> To be a writer is something special. It is to reach, however awkwardly, for the stars, and to move, however haltingly, in that direction. To be a beginner or a semiprofessional or a part-time writer is something just as special as to be a hardened professional.
>
> It's time to reach for the stars!

If this quote inspires you once and for all to fulfill your ambition to become a writer, don't lose your momentum. Read this guide and learn how to fan that flame of creativity you've had burning for such a long time. This book was written for all of you who have often wished to find guidelines that could show you how to get started in fiction or nonfiction, guidelines that are easy to follow *and* informative.

In these chapters you will learn how to choose a subject, how to research it and how to develop it into a professional manuscript. You'll discover how to create a story from what you see and hear all around you, and how to make your characters, plot and dialogue all fit into the mosaic of a good story. You'll find that, with a little know-how, you can become a columnist for a local newspaper—and then try your wings with one of the syndicates. You'll see it's possible for a beginner to do a children's story or even write his memoirs.

As you read this handbook on writing, be aware of one important fact: The author became a professional writer even though she moved more than twenty-five times in twenty years and raised five children. If I accomplished my goal on a part-time basis, so can you!

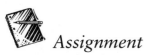 *Assignment*

You've decided that the time has come for you to start that mystery novel you've been thinking about for months. Jot down an opening paragraph now! Don't wait. Communicate. If you prefer a children's story or any other project, good. But start it now!

2 STOP! LOOK! LISTEN!

You've made the decision and you're all set to become a writer, but where will you find the ideas? If you sharpen your five senses, you'll soon have a gold mine that will supply you with writing materials for years to come.

You probably think you are quite observant. But are you really? Whose picture is on the $5 bill? The $10 bill? How many tines are there on a fork? How many columns are in the portico of the White House? What four words appear on every U.S. coin? What kind of trees are in front of your house? Don't despair if you are groping around for the answers. Most of us don't pay enough attention to the world around us. But now that you are planning to become a writer, take time not only to smell the roses, but also to notice their color, texture and shape.

Using their powers of observation, many renowned writers were able to paint word pictures for their readers. In this excerpt from *Look Homeward, Angel,* Thomas Wolfe uses sensory words that make us feel we are actually at the table with Eugene Gant's family, relishing every bite.

At the midday meal, they ate heavily: a huge pot roast of beef, fat buttered lima beans, tender corn smoking on the cob, thick red slabs of sliced tomatoes, rough savory spinach, hot yellow cornbread, flaky biscuits, a deep-dish peach-and-apple cobbler spiced with cinnamon . . .

In the same novel, the author also makes us use our sense of smell when he writes:

[He remembered the smell of] crushed mint leaves and of a wet lilac bush; of magnolia beneath the heavy moon; of dogwood and laurel; of an old caked pipe, and Bourbon rye aged in kegs of charred oak; the sharp smell of tobacco; of imprisoned books; and the cool fern smell near springs; of vanilla in cake dough; and of cloven ponderous cheeses.

Robert Louis Stevenson is another writer who painted pictures. Find a copy of *Treasure Island, Travels With a Donkey* or *Kidnapped* and discover for yourself his ability to observe and describe. Read some of Ernest Hemingway's stories and see how, even in his laconic and direct style, he can still make the reader feel he is part of the action. In his famous short story "Big Two-Hearted River," his use of sensory words makes it possible for everyone to experience Nick Adams's fishing trip: We can smell the coffee brewing; taste the buckwheat cakes; feel the river current against our legs and the pull of the trout on the line; and enjoy the serenity of nature.

Joan Mills, a housewife from New England, has always been interested in this style of writing. When she moved to California, she decided to write an article using sensory words. Here is an excerpt:

Palisades of ageless rock above a sweeping sea. Tall cardon cacti raising branched arms high, guardians of sand and scrub and thorn forests. Jagged mountains against sunset skies supersaturated with pinks, lemon yellows and hot orange . . .

(*Reader's Digest*, July 1979)

High school students are still being asked to describe a penny or a pencil using sensory words, but something new has been added. Some English teachers are trying to stretch their students' imaginations by asking: Which is thinner, night or day? Which weighs more, zero or one? Which is louder, a smile or a frown? After sitting there with blank faces, they come up with answers that are plausible—and outlandish.

Now that you've made a pact with yourself to become more aware of what's going on in the world, you're ready to continue your search for ideas. Frankly, ideas are all around you. At first they will appear to be nebulous—shapeless and shadowy. But before you know it, they will take form and make you eager to communicate your findings. And then a surprising thing will happen—other ideas will pop up as you begin to pound your typewriter or use your computer.

The Newspaper as Idea Source

Have you read your newspaper today? How about reading it again—but this time with a cool, calculating eye toward article and story ideas. Several years ago, I spotted an item in a weekly paper that seemed to leap off the page, enticing me to find out some details.

I took it to my writing class the next morning, and all my students agreed with my reaction. The story revolved around an incident that took place during the French and Indian War in nearby Centreville, Virginia, in April 1755. According to an old legend, Major General Edward Braddock, a British general, was leading a division of Virginia riflemen and six companies of his regiment from Alexandria to Winchester. Suddenly deluged by heavy rains, they became bogged down by mud and obstructed by tree branches. The general decided that the only way to lighten the load was to abandon the $25,000 worth of gold coins he had brought for the payroll. He ordered several soldiers to dismount two cannons, fill them with money and bury them in the mud. They were able to forge ahead, but Braddock was eventually killed, and his papers were sent to England. Years later, an archivist found his report about the gold. Since that time, many people have visited

Centreville to look for the buried treasure. It has never been found.

You can almost guess the rest of this story. Yes, we did venture out to find the two cannons and the gold. After doing a bit of research, we sallied forth one May morning armed with a metal detector, a camera, a map and a picnic lunch. No, we didn't find the coins, but we did discover a painless way to learn American history. For a brief moment, we made a dry subject come alive. And Dody Smith, one of my students, had the satisfaction of seeing her article on our expedition published in the *Arlington News*.

But, you may be thinking, this type of story appears only once in a while. I can assure you that if you read the newspaper more carefully, you'll discover numerous nuggets of information that can be developed into salable material. I decided the other day to go through six newspapers I had on hand and look for items leading to ideas for future articles. These are the ones that appealed to me:

1. People are living longer these days. More and more are reaching the one hundred mark. (What is their secret of longevity?)
2. Hotline volunteers were honored at a luncheon yesterday and given awards. (How are they trained? What are some of the stories they hear? What advice do they give?)
3. An art instructor says she has no qualms about teaching painting to prisoners at the county jail. (What other classes are taught in prison? Are inmates receiving recognition for their work?)
4. For two years now, the residents in a small community have heard a high-pitched keening in the middle of the night. (What other "monsters" have been reported throughout the country? Is there more truth than fiction to all of the stories?)
5. This special test will reveal your psychic powers. (What are some of the new breakthroughs in parapsychology? Why do more and more people believe in psychic phenomena?)
6. The right age to begin thinking about retirement is forty-five (Why should it be done so early? What factors must be considered? Which factor should be at the top of the list?)

These six items generated article ideas, but some of them can also be springboards for short story plots. What if your protagonist, a

9

young woman, becomes a hotline worker and manages to talk a young man out of taking an overdose of drugs by saying all the right things? And in doing so, she also saves herself: She, too, has suicidal tendencies. What if your protagonist, the art teacher, falls in love with one of the prisoners? What if your protagonist, a young man with ESP, falls in love with a beautiful young woman and realizes she is from another world?

But your newspaper has more to offer. Look for the Personals in daily publications—ads placed by people who want to give a message to an individual or a group. Behind each personal ad is a human-interest story. As you read the following four ads I borrowed from an English teacher's notebook, see what thoughts pop up in your mind—and give you instant plots.

STEVE—Please call Paula. Important! 555-8485

WEDDING GOWN, size 14, veil, bridesmaids' dresses, 2 ring pillows. New—never worn. 555-7592

MISS JOHNSON—I have a job for you. Call 555-6788

WANTED—Man with spirit and empty barn. Please contact the Honorable J. Shortell, mayor of Georgetown 1966–1969. 555-4677

These were actual ads, culled from different newspapers. If you are especially interested in fiction, get into the habit of turning to the Personals. You'll find some that are poignant, a few that are humorous—and a number that are downright intriguing. Here is your chance to let your imagination take free rein. Let it run wild: Immediately jot down your ideas for characters and plots and settings.

You can see from these examples that the newspaper is a valuable source of inspiration for writers.

Magazines

Magazines, of course, also lend themselves to article ideas and story lines. Plan now to spend an hour or two in the library whenever you can, browsing through the magazine section. If you haven't done that for a while, you're in for a surprise. You'll find many new publications covering all kinds of subjects, including hobbies, astronomy, history and health. Thumb through them and you'll probably come across some of the following items:

- That "junk" in your attic may be more valuable than you think.
- The moon can be held responsible for some of your moods.
- Some scientists believe that black holes could be the key to the secrets of the universe.
- The Mormons have a lower cancer rate and have fewer heart attacks than the rest of us.
- It's possible that there really was a King Arthur and that he is now resting with his fair queen in Glastonbury Abbey in England.
- Feeling depressed? The experts say you can think your way out of those low periods.
- The "Share-a-Home" concept is gaining momentum with senior citizens throughout the country.
- With a little bit of know-how, you can interpret your own dreams.
- Simple changes in your lifestyle can prolong your life.
- What you can do if diets don't work for you.
- American adults are going back to school and taking courses that range from flower arranging to auto mechanics.
- There is a way to prepare for the "empty nest syndrome."
- Is it true that teachers can't teach?
- How you can prevent an affair.
- How you can survive an audit by the IRS.

What variations on the above themes can you come up with?

As you look through magazines, pay attention to the number of how-to articles. If you have a flair for this kind of writing, you're bound to find a market for a well-written, explicitly detailed piece. Articles that appear almost every month include: How to shop and save; How to make a diet work; How to grow African violets; How to keep from growing old; How to beat inflation; and How to run a yard sale. Even though these features are done again and again, you can add your special know-how to them and make them unique.

If, for example, you have found that your shopping bill is less when you leave your spouse at home, weave that fact into your article. If you used a buddy system on your last diet, tell about it in your article: Describe how it helped you and your best friend lose pounds. If you began to jog at the age of fifty or sixty and became healthier in mind and body, share your secret with the rest of us. If you turned your yard sale into a block affair and made some extra dollars, give us the details.

Books

Books can also be a font of ideas for articles and fillers. If you are interested in writing inspirational material, for example, reread *The Power of Positive Thinking* by Norman Vincent Peale. Why was his book so successful? Why is it still read today? What are your suggestions for positive thinking? If you read *The Cosmic Connection* by Carl Sagan, you'll not only have an update on our nine planets, but a description of Venus that fits one concept of hell. Dr. Sagan says that this planet is "sizzling, choking, sulfurous and red." Do you believe there is a hell? Where is it? Is it a place or a state of mind? During the past ten years, hell hasn't been discussed too often in the churches. With the renewed interest in religion, this may be the time to do a feature on this topic for a magazine.

Biographies of famous men and women have much to offer the beginning writer. A few years ago, I began to read profiles of the writers I admired and of a few other heroes. I was amazed at the wealth of information I acquired in just a few months. As my note-book became crammed with facts, I wondered what I could do with them. A short time later, I spied a notice on a bulletin board at the high school where I was substituting. A publisher in Michigan was looking for stories about famous people or events to use for his educational publications in elementary grades. I sent him vignettes on the lives of Mary Shelley, Nathan Hale, Robert Louis Stevenson, Jules Verne and Christopher Columbus. He liked the way I started each story—strong leads that caught the attention of young readers. He also approved of the intriguing facts I used:

Mary Shelley wrote her tale of horror based on a nightmare she had on a stormy night; Nathan Hale was probably turned in by his cousin; Jules Verne was a hundred years ahead of his time and "went" to the moon in 1865; Columbus was tall, redheaded and freckled; Robert Louis Stevenson gave away his birthday (legally) to the daughter of a friend, whose birthday was on Christmas Day, so she could have two days for presents like other children.

Are you in the middle of another book besides this one? If you are, don't be surprised if an idea for an article or story suddenly storms into your consciousness and won't leave. Jot it down at once. When Midge Papich, one of my students, read *Nicholas and Alexandra* by R.K. Massie, she was so impressed with the Easter gifts the czars of Russia gave their wives that she decided to write about them. These were the famous jewel-encrusted eggs made by Fabergé between 1885 and 1917. Each one of them contained a surprise, ranging from a gold miniature of the palace to a ruby pendant. Midge did her research, and on Easter morning of that year her article appeared in the *Washington Post*. When Muriel Mckenna came across a reference to the history of gloves in a book she was reading, she wanted to know more. She, too, did some research, wrote a feature and had it published in a weekly paper.

Now here's a delightful way to search for ideas. Have you seen a copy of *The People's Almanac* (Doubleday, 1975)? Compiled by Irving Wallace and his son David Wallechinsky, it claims to be "the first reference book ever prepared to be read for pleasure." It's equal to ten books in size, so you won't be able to tuck it under your arm or into your purse. But you'll want to. Some of its facts you'll want to research are:

- Photographs taken by Skylab may have located the remains of Noah's Ark.
- Adolf Hitler owned 8,960 acres of land in Colorado.
- There is more than $4 billion in lost or buried treasure scattered throughout the United States.
- Guards at the Alamos, Mexico, jail have to serve out the sentences of any prisoners who escape while the guards are on duty.
- Harvey Kennedy invented the shoelace and made $2.5 million on his patent.

The book contains many detailed articles on every subject imaginable. You will be interested to know that freelancers contributed many of the stories—and were listed in the credits in the front of the book. Dody Smith, who wrote about our search for Braddock's gold, was assigned to do a follow-up on what happened to the *Bounty* mutineers. And there on page 516 is her fascinating account of what she discovered about Pitcairn Island.

Television

In addition to newspapers, magazines and books, writers can watch TV for ideas to use in writing fiction and nonfiction. In soap operas and movies, they can get plot ideas and pick up mannerisms for their heroes and heroines. Tom, for example, can show his frustrations by drumming his fingers on his desk. Carol can show how loving she is by giving quick hugs to her friends. Jerry has the habit of tapping the love of his life gently on the nose when he is making a point and believes he is right.

Television is also important for writers when they are trying to write dialogue. TV dialogue is usually fast and snappy: It's the way people talk. Write some of it down. If there is a movie similar to what you are writing, rent it and play it over and over in your VCR, repeating the lines out loud. Always say the dialogue in your stories or novels out loud. Tom Clancy says, "Speak your dialogue out loud. If it sounds like the way real people talk, write it down."

Writers interested in doing biographies can also make use of television. Some of the cable networks feature famous men and women of the past and the present, using intriguing facts and carefully researched material that may motivate you to do a biography on your own. Sometimes a transcript is available for a nominal sum—and worth sending for.

Other Idea Sources

Other ideas for writing can stem from being a good listener. From now on, pay more attention to what your friends and relatives are saying. Not too long ago, a friend told me about the beer bread she was planning to make to go with her chili supper that night. We were standing in line at the supermarket, and before long she had quite an audience. She said that she had gotten the recipe from an all-night disc jockey who mentioned it casually to fill some airtime. All you need is 3 cups of self-rising flour, 3 tablespoons of sugar, and 1 can (12 ounces) of beer. Mix the ingredients lightly. Pour at once into a well-greased pan. Bake in a 375° oven for forty-five minutes. Voila! You have not only a unique loaf of bread, but also a great conversation piece at the table. I wasn't surprised when the recipe appeared in print the following week. Someone had been shrewd enough to realize that this recipe would find a ready market—and was right on target.

If you become a good listener, you may even hear some unusual stories and legends. Stashed away in the ragbag of my mind is a tale told in Europe in which the devil takes human form once a year for twenty-four hours and can appear anywhere he wishes. Only last week at a writers' meeting, an Irishman said that in his country there is a legend that God takes human form once a year for a day and night, and visits a different country each time. What if God and the devil both took the same day and met? What if a young woman was seated in a restaurant or inn across from a handsome stranger and found herself almost mesmerized by his eyes? Who would he be? Satan or God?

Ideas can also come from your family life. Have you survived a divorce? Are you a new stepparent? Have you gone back to work after twenty years, or are you going back to school to get a degree? Have you volunteered to be a surrogate mother? Has your son or daughter become involved with drugs? Are you dreading the whole idea of retirement? Is your family life happy? (If it is, please share your secret with those people who believe that the family unit will soon be a thing of the past.)

Holidays can also furnish subjects to write about. Check newspapers and magazines, and save the items that tell about the origins of Halloween, Thanksgiving, Yom Kippur or Christmas. After you do your research, include those tidbits that add a special touch to your filler or article. Did you know that Christmas once was banned in Boston? Did you know that the first Thanksgiving lasted for three days?

Do you have a hobby? Write about it. The men and women in my writing classes during the past fourteen years have turned their expertise in cooking, magic, book collecting, gardening, poetry, writing, travel and Virginia history into bylines and pocket money. Wade Fleetwood's hobby of collecting grains of sand from all over the world is always a conversation starter. Not only has he written it up, but he has been interviewed and featured in several publications. He keeps the grains of sand in glass vials; the reporters are fascinated by the colors, which range from a blush pink to a charcoal gray.

Can you remember your dreams? Good! You already have a source for ideas for your writing. But since dreams vanish so quickly, stumble over to your notebook when you awaken and scribble some key words that will help you reconstruct what happened. It is said that Robert Louis Stevenson could dream plots at will. His famous story *Dr. Jekyll and Mr. Hyde* came to him one night almost in its entirety, and he sat down the next morning and wrote it all down. Samuel Coleridge's poem "Kubla Khan" also came from a dream. But there is a footnote to this story. As he was sitting at his desk, scribbling away, someone knocked on the door. When he returned to his writing, he couldn't remember how his dream ended. If you read the poem, you will see that it is unfinished. And if you have a nightmare now and then, hang on to it. As noted previously, Mary Shelley wrote *Frankenstein* after she experienced a terrifying vision on a stormy night.

Now that you have finished reading this chapter, it is time for you to begin writing. Choose one of the subjects listed on these pages. Add to it from your memories or expertise. Round it out with information from your local library. Nurture it day after day in your thoughts. The time will come when you will want to get it all down on paper and share it with the world.

But you can reach that point sooner if you start now!

 Assignment

Write up four intriguing items that caught your eye in your daily paper today. (If you can't find four items, make it a point to be more observant.)

3 TOOLS OF THE TRADE

Whether you write fiction or nonfiction, you will need certain tools to help you become a selling writer. Buy yourself a good dictionary, a thesaurus and a set of encyclopedias. If you use a computer, it may have a dictionary and thesaurus, and even a spell-check system. Later, you can add *Webster's Collegiate Dictionary*, which contains biographies and geographical names at the back, or *Funk and Wagnall's Standard College Dictionary*.

If you don't have a set of encyclopedias at home, this is the time to scout around and buy one. It's important to own a set, because it will save you time. Whenever an idea for a story or article grabs you, your A-to-Z books are right there to give you the basic information you need. You can then go to the library and find books and articles on the subject. Years ago, I bought the *World Book*, and use them again and again. I like the format: I can find things quickly, and it is easy to understand. (A footnote: You can get *World Book* on CDs, and a number of other encyclopedias are also available in this format.)

Armed with these basic books, you should be able to turn out a credible manuscript. But the more you write, the more critical you'll become of what you are producing. You'll worry about the mechanics of writing, and wonder if your commas are all in the right place. The best little paperback around is *The Elements of Style* by William Strunk, Jr., and E.B. White. It was originally written by Professor

Strunk when he taught English at Cornell University more than seventy years ago. E.B. White was a student there, and found himself greatly impressed by the professor and his course. In 1957, he was commissioned by the MacMillan Publishing Company to make some revisions to the text. (In addition to being a master stylist himself, he was also a humorist, an essayist and the author of *Charlotte's Web* and *Stuart Little*.) He added a chapter of his own, which lends a special touch to Strunk's rules of rhetoric.

Both of these men have made us aware of style. Some English teachers in high school give out certain paragraphs to their students and ask them to identify the writers. Here are two short paragraphs. Can you identify the author of each?

It was late and everyone had left the café except an old man who sat in the shadow the leaves of the tree made against the electric light. In the daytime the street was dusty, but at night the dew settled the dust, and the old man liked to sit late because he was deaf and now at night it was quiet and he felt the difference.

Then, in the cool long glade of yard that stretched four hundred feet behind the house, he planted trees and grapevines. And whatever he touched in that rich fortress of his soul sprang into golden life: As the years passed, the fruit trees—the peach, the plum, the cherry, the apple—grew great and bent beneath their clusters. His grapevines thickened into brawny ropes of brown and coiled down the high wire fences of his lot. . . . And flowers grew in rioting glory in his yard—the velvet-leaved nasturtium slashed with a hundred tawny dyes, the rose, the snowball, the red-capped tulip and the lily.

The first piece was done by Ernest Hemingway. You can readily see that his prose was laconic: He could express himself in a few words. Thomas Wolfe, on the other hand, uses rich, lush prose to describe the fruit trees, grapevines and flowers in his yard.

This contrast in writing will make you aware that an author can be recognized by his style. Terse? Brief? Flowery? Poetic? You will develop your own style as you begin to write.

The Elements of Style will teach you many other things. Five important ones are:

- Write in a way that comes naturally.
- Work from a suitable design—an outline.
- Write with nouns and verbs.
- Avoid the use of qualifiers.
- Omit needless words.

E.B. White emphasizes the fact that William Strunk told his students over and over that every good writer must omit unnecessary words. This rule is one of the most difficult to follow. Many beginning writers—and some professionals—find it painful to go through a manuscript and cut out words and phrases that took time and effort to produce. But you can do it. Keep telling yourself that even the best writers find it agonizing to streamline their work. Eventually, you'll make every word count.

The best training I've every had along these lines was years ago when I wrote 365 radio scripts for a syndicate in Kansas City, Missouri. Each script, which had to tell something about a day of the year, was only sixty seconds long. My producer showed me how to take details about a holiday, an event or a famous person and make them into a dramatic minute. There were times when I thought it just couldn't be done and wished I had never signed the contract for the job. But the challenge forced me to choose every word carefully and in such a way that the listener was impressed with what he heard. My best one-minute script read:

(June 18)

The cold, penetrating rain slashed against the general's face, and he shivered as he turned up the collar of his greatcoat. It had been raining for hours, and when dawn came, he decided not to drag his artillery across the soggy fields. It was a decision that would be recorded in history forever. Napoleon Bonaparte, one of the greatest military geniuses of all time, who "aimed his army like a pistol," waited for a sun that never appeared. At 11:30 on the morning of June 18, he

19

ordered his French troops to attack the Duke of Wellington's army in the Belgian town of Waterloo. But while Napoleon tarried with his men, Marshall von Blucher and his weary Prussian soldiers had slogged through the mud to reinforce the British military units. Napoleon's defeat was so overwhelming that when someone now suffers a disastrous setback, we say he has "met his Waterloo."

From now on, use vivid verbs and concrete nouns instead of all those adjectives and adverbs. Professor Strunk said it first; it's become a cardinal rule in my class and one that I repeat often. If you need some coaching in vivid verbs, read the sports page in your daily newspaper. There you'll find such things as

Maryland Rips Vanderbilt

Middies Stun Washington

Royals Rout Yanks

SMU Rocks Texas

Astros Whip Phillies

John Harkes Blasts the Los Angeles Galaxy

If you're a poetry buff, you'll also find some vivid verbs in your favorite poems. These four lines from one of John Donne's religious sonnets are a good example:

Batter my heart, three-personed God; for you
As yet but knock, breathe, shine, and seek to mend
That I may rise and stand, o'erthroe me and bend
Your force to break, blow, burn and make me new.

From now on, train yourself to use action verbs. Don't always have your character *walk* into a room: Have him *shuffle, stagger, saunter, swagger* or *slink* in. But one word of caution: Don't go overboard on this kind of writing. Reading the sports page and poetry should only be a training exercise. As for the verb *said*, there's no reason why you can't use *grumbled*, *called* or *shouted*, but do it in moderation.

And what about the use of concrete nouns? This may be a little more difficult to do, but once you get into the habit of doing it, your troubles are over. Concrete nouns are useful in description, because the reader can picture them in his mind. For example, if you simply say that your grandson raises flowers for a hobby, it doesn't mean much. But if you tell us that he raises lavender orchids, we can see them immediately. Whenever you can, turn that house into a cabin, that tree into an elm, that boat into a tramp steamer and that cat into a gray-striped tabby.

Don't abandon all of your adverbs and adjectives, but do choose them carefully. Make every one count. The right adjective can be another tool in your writing kit. If you're describing an apple, it's much more effective if you tell us that it is wormy instead of that it is red. If your writing seems to have too many qualifiers, cut out *very*, *pretty*, *big* and *little*. But if qualifiers are necessary once in a while, use more colorful synonyms. Something *big* can be *grand*, *gigantic* or *massive*. Something *little* can be *diminutive*, *wee* or *tiny*.

Boosting Your Vocabulary

Improving your vocabulary is another way to make your writing more dynamic. There are over 600,000 words in the English language, but even the most learned people seldom use more than 24,000 different words during the course of their lives. The more words you acquire, the easier it will be to find the right ones to express yourself. The best way to increase your vocabulary is to read. Whenever a strange word pops up, reach for the dictionary.

If you were asked to give the ten most beautiful words in the English language, what would your answer be? According to *The New Webster's Encyclopedic Dictionary*, they are

lullaby	soul
murmuring	golden
noble	glow
slumber	twilight
melody	home

You must admit that these words are pleasant to the ear, but why not work on a list of your own? Thumb through some of your favorite passages in your favorite books and jot down those nouns and adjectives that appeal to you. Watch for others as you read current magazines or novels: Add them to your list. You may even want to collect words you find ugly or jarring. Become a wordsmith, an expert on words, and when you do, be ready for an exhilarating and exciting experience. Nathaniel Hawthorne said, "Words—so innocent and powerless as they are, as standing in a dictionary, how potent for good and evil they become, in the hands of one who knows how to combine them." Here is your chance to learn how to choose the right combination and communicate your ideas to the world.

A brand new tool for writers is America Online Writing Club. If you are new to the writing field, click on "Welcome Newcomers." It will take you to a page with twelve topics to choose from, including "articles," "romance" and "the business of writing." Later, you can enter the World Wide Web and use any of twenty-five online services, including how to find an agent, workshops, contests, poetry and so on. And on this information highway, you can tune into other reference sources, including the latest in dictionaries and encyclopedias.

Building Your Reference Library

The basic tools I've discussed will give you the necessary assists in becoming a professional writer. Here are some "nice to have" reference works you can pick up as your checks come in:

- *The Careful Writer*, by Theodore M. Bernstein, is a delightful book that tells you such things as when to use *farther* and *further* and how to avoid split infinitives. Mr. Bernstein's style is witty and easy to understand.
- *The Columbia-Viking Desk Encyclopedia* is a one-volume book with condensed information on an amazing number of subjects. It's the best of its kind and is a great time-saver. The paperback edition is also a money-saver.
- *The Reader's Encyclopedia*, by William Rose Benet, will hold you entranced with its information about authors, places,

characters, literary works and even words. I can't remember when I latched on to it, but every time I bring my two copies into my classroom, my students spirit them away to devour some of their fascinating facts. Since I began to immerse myself in its pages, I have learned that it's quite possible that the Fountain of Youth is on Bimini Island in the Bahamas; the Holy Grail came into the possession of Joseph of Arimathea, and eventually was passed down to Sir Galahad, his last descendant; it's possible that Pontius Pilate became a Christian and repented of his sins; and that Cervantes was captured by Barbary pirates and held as a slave in Algiers for five years. The subjects are arranged in dictionary form. Turn to any page and you'll pick up an idea for research or for a story.

- *Bartlett's Familiar Quotations* will wend its way into your writing more than you think. There will be times when you are scurrying around for a phrase that will add a special touch or accent to your article, or you have to track down who said this or that on a certain subject. It is arranged chronologically by authors quoted and also has a key-word index. There are several collections of quotations on the market, but this is the best.

- *The World Almanac* will supply you with information on events of the previous year, statistics on populations, profiles of famous people, facts about countries and more. You may also want to buy *The New York Times Encyclopedic Almanac*, which contains such things as a calendar of events of a hundred years ago and a list of endangered wildlife.

  Many of these reference books can be found at your library. But in addition to the encyclopedias, dictionaries and almanacs in the library's collection, you'll find a wealth of material waiting for you the minute you walk in the door. Get acquainted with your reference librarian, who can point out the following:

- *The Reader's Guide to Periodical Literature* is an index of articles in more than 160 magazines published in the United States. It is an excellent source of current information and will save you all kinds of time. As soon as you have an idea for an article, check this guide to see what has already been written on the subject. Author and subject entries are combined in one alphabetical index, and each listing gives the details necessary to find the articles in the magazines. A list of abbreviations used in the guide appears in the front of every issue. *The Reader's Guide* is published twice a month, with cumulative issues appearing at the end of every year.

- *Who's Who in America, Who's Who in the World* and *Who Was Who in America* will help you find information on men and women of today and yesterday. And you'll enjoy looking up facts in *Current Biography*, which will reveal that Julia Child, the TV cook, wanted to be a spy during World War II, and that Jean-Claude Killy started skiing when he was only three years old.

- Joseph Kane's *Famous First Facts* will fill you in on all kinds of unusual information, including tidbits on the first balloon, the first ice cream sundae and the first library. Kane's *Facts About the Presidents* will not only give you details on the men in the White House, but will also draw comparisons among our leaders along the lines of religion, their ages when they took office and so on.

- Frank Magill's *Masterplots* provides plot summaries of more than two thousand novels, plays and essays. His *Masterpieces of World Philosophy* will, in summary form, supply you with facts about the major philosophies and religions, ranging from Plato to Sartre.

While you are at the library, familiarize yourself with the books on creative writing. You'll find material on how to write fillers, articles, columns, short stories, novels, nonfiction books and children's stories. Now is the time to pick up a copy of *Writer's Digest* and *The Writer*, two magazines that provide advice and up-to-date market listings. They will also suggest a number of books the library doesn't have on hand, so that you can build your own reference collection around the category in which you are interested.

Before you leave the library, ask one of the librarians to show you where the *vertical file* is. It is often overlooked, and yet it may have just what you have been looking for. It usually contains information on current topics: pamphlets published by government agencies, museums and industries; newspaper clippings and photographs of important events; local history, etc. These items are filed standing on edge and are often found in a big drawer in the main room.

If your library is a large one, you can become acquainted with *The New York Times Index*: It will prove invaluable in your research projects. This index is bound in annual volumes and is arranged chronologically under subject headings with date, page and column references. By checking this index, you will get the gist of what the *Times* printed about your subject; later, you can go back to the files either in bound form or on microfilm to read the articles themselves. If your library does not have this index, call a nearby university.

Two books that you'll find helpful in any kind of research that you do are *Finding Facts Fast* by Alden Todd and *The Writer's Ultimate Research Guide* by Ellen Metter (Writer's Digest Books). The first one is based on methods used by librarians, scholars, investigative reporters and detectives; the second is a new book filled with lists of books (1,700), online resources and periodicals.

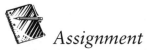 *Assignment*

Think of a topic that has always intrigued you. Check it out in your encyclopedia, and then go to the library to find books and periodicals that will provide details to round out your article.

4 TRY A FILLER FIRST

Now that you are inspired to put words to paper, what should you write? How should you begin to communicate your thoughts, ideas and observations to the world? "Great oaks from little acorns grow" is a trite but true statement: It really is a good idea to start out with short items, or fillers.

Defining Fillers

What exactly is a filler? At one time it was an item used to fill the end of a column at the bottom of a page in a newspaper or magazine. Although this is still true to a certain extent today, the filler has come into its own. Editors realize that their readers look for those little items that intrigue them or make them chuckle. Some writers send out two, three or more fillers a week to make pocket money. Concentrating on this field alone, you can make enough money to pay for a mini-vacation twice a year.

A filler can range from a phrase to about 500 words. It can be a pun, a quip, an epigram, a household hint, a food fact, a footnote to history, light verse, a recipe, a joke, a puzzle, a how-to hint, a daffy definition, a child's bright saying, an anecdote or a typographical error. On the following pages, you'll find examples of the different kinds of fillers: Don't be surprised if they jog your memory and your imagination. Be sure to jot down ideas for fillers whenever they occur. Don't depend on remembering tidbits of information: They are elusive, and some never come back.

If you have a flair for creating a play on words, capitalize on it; you will find a ready market out there. *Reader's Digest* is one of the most popular markets for this kind of filler—and the most difficult to get into. But aim for this market from time to time. Here are two fillers sent in by freelancers:

Grammar's reach should exceed its grasp or what's a metaphor?
(George O. Ludcke, *Reader's Digest*, May 1996)

There's no mistaking that voice; it's like bourbon over sandpaper.
(Christopher Buckley, *Reader's Digest*, July 1996)

Would you like to try a quip? This is a clever or witty remark, such as:

People are like plants—some go to seed with age, others go to pot.
(*Senior Scribes*, June 1981)

Plenty of people have a good aim in life, but a lot of them don't know when to pull the trigger.
(*Senior Scribes*, June 1981)

Pollution costs us millions; grime doesn't pay.
(*Senior Scribes*, June 1981)

An epigram, according to the dictionary, is "any witty, ingenious or pointed saying tersely expressed." It is a slice of life reaching a wide group of readers. Without a doubt, Ben Franklin found this kind of writing easy to do, and his *Poor Richard's Almanac* is full of pointed sayings.

God helps them that help themselves.

Those have a short Lent who owe Money to be paid at Easter.

27

An up-to-date epigram comes from the pen of humorist Sam Levenson, who wrote:

A sweater is a garment that a child wears because his mother is cold.

If you have a penchant for light verse, cultivate it! A number of magazines are looking for it, including the *Saturday Evening Post*, *Good Housekeeping*, *Playboy*, *Woman's Day*, *Yankee*, *Ebony* and *Reader's Digest*. Richard Armour is a master in this form of writing—these four lines made him famous:

> Going to Extremes
> Shake and shake
> the catsup bottle.
> None will come,
> And then a lot'll.

(*Light Armour*, McGraw-Hill, 1954)

Household hints can usually find a ready market, and they are fun to write. Draw upon your own experiences, and thumb through magazines and newspapers for ideas. Check with members of your family: They may have old almanacs around or a family recipe that dates back many years. Nostalgia is "in." Put your memory to work and capitalize on it. What made your Thanksgiving dinner extra special? What did your Aunt Jennie do to make her children's parties so successful? What was your Uncle Joe's remedy for soothing poison ivy? What did your mother concoct for the racking cough you had after a cold?

If you think these bits of information are trivial, think again. Begin to collect them now. They may lead to something big. A case in point: In 1979, two enterprising women, Mary Ellen Pinkham and Pearl Higginbotham, published a book of ways to solve common household problems. They called it *Mary Ellen's Best Helpful Hints*. It was a huge success and was reprinted for a number of years. Here are a few of their tips that are unique and very helpful.

28

• Store cottage cheese upside down. It will keep longer.

- To keep lettuce fresh in the refrigerator, store it in paper bags instead of cellophane.
- To clean eyeglasses without leaving streaks, use a drop of vinegar or vodka on each lens.
- When postage stamps are stuck together, place them in the freezer.
- For your plants, use water at room temperature. Let the water stand for a day to get rid of chlorine. Better yet, use old, fizzless club soda—it has just the right chemicals to add vigor to your plants.
- If there's a bee—or any winged insect—in the house, reach for the hairspray. This stiffens their wings and immobilizes them immediately.

(*Mary Ellen's Best of Helpful Hints,* Warner Books, 1979)

This is a category that intrigues me; I have been collecting similar items for years. Mine aren't as clever as Mary Ellen's, but some of mine may motivate you to write down some of yours and get you started in this category:

- Forget to take the meat out of the freezer before you left the house for the day? No problem if you have a microwave. If not, shred the meat on a rough cabbage shredder—hold the frozen block in one hand as if it were a head of cabbage.
- An apple corer is a good tool to use when transplanting tiny seedlings; it does less damage than a trowel, and makes handling the delicate plants much easier.
- Raw eggs spilled on the kitchen floor make a gooey mess, but if you cover them with salt for twenty minutes, you'll have no trouble sweeping them up.
- A few cloves in the corners of your shelves and cupboards will discourage ants and give your cabinets a spicy smell.
- If a piece of Great-Aunt Margaret's tea set is cracked but not broken, boil it in milk for forty-five minutes. The crack will disappear and the china will be stronger.
- Meat can be successfully reheated for a late guest if it is placed in a heavy skillet, covered with lettuce leaves and a lid, and then heated in a moderate oven for a short time.

29

There is a renewed interest in the culinary arts lately because of the emphasis on diet and health issues, and food facts will find a ready market in magazines and newspapers. But before you go hunting down the facts, test the market with a recipe. Do the guests always come back for more at your buffet suppers? Do they always ask for the recipe? Is it fairly inexpensive? Write it up and send it off. You will find food facts when you least expect them. I came across this tidbit in a daily newspaper a few years ago.

The *largest* single dish in the world is roasted camel, prepared occasionally for Bedouin wedding feasts: Cooked eggs are stuffed into fish, the fish are stuffed into cooked chickens, the chickens are stuffed into a roasted sheep carcass and the sheep is stuffed into a whole camel.

Are you a history buff? You may want to collect items that revolve around historical figures or events. If you have always been a great admirer of Robert E. Lee, write up the fact that at the beginning of the Civil War, he was asked to lead the Union troops. If you have always been intrigued with Cleopatra, do a filler that describes her as a fascinating conversationalist, a first-rate military strategist and a remarkable actress, instead of a wanton seductress. If you have some expertise on the Revolutionary War, write an anecdote about Samuel Adam's dog, who bit only Redcoats.

Footnotes to history make interesting reading. During the Bicentennial, I wrote over two hundred radio scripts in which I pretended to be a journalist who lived two centuries ago. Later, I wrote fillers and articles, telling my readers that dinner at Mount Vernon began promptly at 3 P.M.; George Washington's favorite wine was Madeira; dessert was usually strawberry tarts or whiskey pie; the general had only one ambition—to become the country's leading agriculturalist; two hundred years ago, backgammon was popular; only seven planets were known to exist; and the mint julep and the cocktail came into being.

Speaking of backgammon, how's your game? Do you know anything about its origin? Do some research, and you'll be amazed at what you'll find. Its history can be traced back five thousand years.

It was fashionable in ancient Greece and Rome: Plato mentions it, and the Emperor Caligula reportedly cheated at it. Cleopatra, by the way, was a whiz at the game. If you like games and cards, find out something about them, and your filler material will almost write itself.

How are you at puzzles? If you can compose a crossword from scratch, you'll have no trouble finding a market. But since they are difficult to do, you may want to try your hand at a similar kind of filler:

On December 17, 1903, Orville Wright made a brief but historical trip by plane. Each of the following fictional characters also made a famous trip—but by what means of transportation?

1. Casey Jones	1. Train
2. Cinderella	2. Coach
3. Hans Brinker	3. Ice skates
4. The Joad family	4. Truck
5. Huckleberry Finn	5. Raft
6. Phileas Fogg	6. Balloon
7. Eliza	7. Ice floes
8. Winken, Blinken and Nod	8. Wooden shoe

(*Modern Maturity*, Dec.–Jan. 1971)

Are you getting ready to travel? Taking a trip to England? Make sure to stop at the British Museum in London to see the mummy, said to be five thousand years old, of an Egyptian woman. Her fingernails, painted dark red, will give you an intriguing little filler. You'll also pick up filler material if you sign up for the tour that takes you to haunted castles. Before you go, see what you can find out about King Harold and Lawrence of Arabia. The ghosts of both of them go wandering about, according to townsfolk.

Are you the joker in your crowd? Capitalize on your talent: Write down the jokes you do so well. A word of caution: Study the market and observe the way jokes are written up. Notice how they begin, how they build, and how everything depends on the right kind of punch line.

Is astronomy your hobby? Share your findings with your earthling friends—tell them about the awesome universe. More and more people are becoming interested in the heavens and outer space. Tell them that we all came from the stars a long time ago. Reveal to them that there are at least a hundred billion other galaxies whirling through space—there *must* be different kinds of life out there, whether we want to believe it or not. And what are black holes? Can you explain them in layman's language? All of these items can be written up as fillers or articles.

Have you always been interested in the signs of the zodiac? What do you really know about it? Have you read Linda Goodman's books on astrology? She'll tell you so many intimate details about your life that you'll believe she's your alter ego. Here's your chance to do some fascinating research. You'll discover that it all began more than five thousand years ago in the Persian Gulf area—and you'll come across many intriguing facts that will lend themselves to filler material and articles. Do you know why there are twelve people on a jury? The story is told that many years ago, a defendant was sure that the only way he could get a fair trial was to have all the signs of the zodiac represented. Find out what famous people in history had their own astrologers. Who are the VIPs of today who don't make a move without their charts being read? Why is this pseudoscience so popular today?

It's possible that you are a collector of strange and unusual facts. If they are not too far out and make good reading, keep on collecting them. You should be able to find a market if they sound something like the following:

- It takes seventeen muscles to smile and forty-three muscles to frown.
- The average heart beats 100,000 times every day.
- Taking a bite of another person's hamburger is against the law in Oklahoma.
- In New Jersey, you can be arrested for slurping your soup in a restaurant.

If Christmas is one of your favorite holidays, you should be able to find a market for your items every year. Do you know some folklore about animals, the weather or decorations? There is much of it relating to December 25, and people like to read about it again and again. Do some browsing at the library and find out what happened to the Three Wise Men after they left Bethlehem. Find out why Christmas was banned in Boston during the colonial period.

Be sure to write your fillers and mail them to the magazine at least six months ahead of time. (All seasonal material should be done this way.) You'll find it strange to think about Christmas on a sunny day in June, but before long, it will seem the natural thing to do.

Are you superstitious? Then you'll enjoy collecting material aimed for Halloween or Friday the 13th. But don't be content with the ordinary superstitions: walking under ladders, avoiding black cats or spilling salt at the table. Try to find family superstitions that will make interesting reading. When my students reminisced, they came up with unusual ones: If you go out one door, come back in through another; when stirring batter, stir in only one direction; don't ever have two clocks ticking in the same room; make sure you never put a hat on a bed. Do some research on Friday the 13th: Most people don't know why it is associated with bad luck. You'll be surprised by the details you'll find.

And while you're checking with your family about superstitions, see if they can remember any quotes and profound sayings of Uncle George or Grandpa Miller. Look up the philosophical lines that have appealed to you through the years, and write them down in your notebook. *Reader's Digest* publishes this kind of material, but try the *Christian Science Monitor* or *Grit* magazine first.

A new kind of filler has been appearing lately, and some of you may have a flair for this kind of writing. Do you find yourself enjoying the bumper stickers you see as you drive along the highways? An old one that impressed me said "Wise men still seek Him." A new one that made me grin said, "I finally got it all, together—and now I don't know where I put it." Be on the lookout for other signs, and try doing some of your own. It's definitely a growing market.

33

You may even find an idea for a filler in the preface of a book. If you pick up a copy of Walter Lord's *A Night to Remember*, you'll discover a story within a story. In 1898, a struggling writer by the name of Morgan Robertson wrote a novel about a luxury liner full of rich people enjoying themselves. Robertson created a tragedy: The ship struck an iceberg and went down in the murky waters of the Atlantic on a cold April night. Many lives were lost on a steamer that was supposed to be unsinkable. Does all of this sound familiar? It should. On April 10, 1912, a real ship left Southhampton, England, on her maiden voyage to New York. She, too, struck an iceberg, and more than 1,400 lives were lost. She was called the *Titanic*; the imaginary one was named *Titan*. It is ironic to note that Robertson's story didn't make much of an impression on the reading public. In fact, his tales of the sea only won the recognition they deserved years after he had died.

Do you have a pet peeve? Do you know someone who has done good in your community? Were you helped by a stranger when your car fell apart on the highway? Do you have a poignant story to tell about your old tiger cat or the mutt you recently acquired? Did your young son or granddaughter regale your guests with a funny remark or a shrewd observation? Do you have an anecdote that is bizarre or humorous or startling? These subjects are also grist for the filler mill. Another source, of course, is your public library. Here you can go through some of the encyclopedias and other tomes—but be careful. Don't wind up with a filler that sounds stilted and dull. Accept the challenge to make it sound exciting and unusual: Put your creative talents to work. While you are browsing, check the magazines for filler markets. Become acquainted with new publications. Look for magazines that seem to suit your style and material.

A Writer Sells a Filler

In 1987, Ellen Braaf had a puzzled look on her face when she left my class. "I'm still not sure what a filler is," she said. When she stopped at a supermarket to pick up some soap for her washing machine, an idea popped into her mind. She wrote it up, sent it out to *Soap Opera Digest* and sold it for $225. (She brought the check to class.) Here is her delightful tidbit.

Dawn had a Top Job as an account executive in an advertising agency. She worked like a human Dynamo, but All her talent couldn't Safeguard her job.

One fateful afternoon, Sol, her boss, called her into his office. She didn't like the Tone of his voice as he said, "Bon Ami, you will Gain a lot if you Snuggle up to me . . . if you get my Dreft!" He Tackled her behind his desk. "You know you want to Cling Free to me. You think I'm Fab," he leered.

"That's a Lysol!" Dawn sobbed. "I won't Pine-Sol without you."

She may not have been as pure as Ivory Snow, but Dawn wanted no part of him. She called out an S.O.S., but no one came to her Rescue. Twisting free of his grasp, she made a mad Dash for the door.

After that, there was no happiness in her Life. "Buoy, if I could only find a new job, I could make a Fresh Start," she thought, then Dialed the number of Bor A Teem, a public relations firm with an exciting job opening. With a Final Touch to her makeup, she marched into their offices. As Lux would have it, they hired her on the spot. She was able to Bounce back.

In love with her new job, after several months Dawn realized that she had also fallen in love with . . . Jergens, the company president. She longed for him to take her in his Arm and Hammer his lips to hers. She ached for his Caress. But he was a Calgon of virtue. Finally, she decided that she didn't want to Coast through life anymore. "This is a new Era for women," she told herself. "Maybe I'll set a new Trend." Her fear Vanished, and as Bold as you please she strode into his office to turn the Tide on their relationship.

"I think you're Fantastic!" she cooed. "You're a Tough Act to follow. Will you marry me?" Wisking her into his arms, he replied, "Yes, I Lava you, too."

The honeymoon was a Joy, and nine months later, at 409 in the morning, she gave birth to Ajax, their first son. Filled with love, he bent over and kissed her forehead. "My little Dove," he said, "this special day will remain a Vivid memory all my life. Our child was born with Lestoil than I ever imagined. What do you say to more children, my love . . . dozens and dozens of them?"

She cradled the baby's Downy head in her arms. "No Comet," she sighed.

(Soap Opera Digest, March 11, 1987)

Then in 1989 and in 1995, two of my senior retirees had their fillers published in Encore! Encore!, a senior publication in Arlington.

How great it is at the end of the day,
To sit in my chair and be able to say
"Look what I did."
It matters not what I have done,
For just the doing is part of the fun.
It may be work or it may be play.
But it's good to rest and be able to say
"Look what I did."
Life is too short to fritter away,
Without something to show at the end of each day.
It matters not what it may be—
Whatever I've done is a part of me
And I can point with pride and say
"Look what I have done today."

Betty Knight
(Encore! Encore!, Dec.–Jan. 1995)

Some cannibals captured a traveler who was trekking in the jungle. They took him back to their remote village to cook him for their chief's dinner. Just before lighting the fire, the cook asked, "What did you do in your country?" "I was an editor," the traveler replied. "Well," said the cook, "You're getting promoted. You're about to become an editor-in-chief."

Lyla Colburn Shealy
(*Encore! Encore!*, April–May 1989)

Getting Organized

Buy a small notebook for all your jottings. No writer can depend entirely on memory. This tool should fit into a purse or pocket. It doesn't sound like much, but you won't be able to live without it from now on. Take it with you on planes, trains and buses. Use it in the doctor's office or the dentist's waiting room. If you decide to concentrate on filler writing, this kind of notebook is a must—and will pay dividends within a few months.

As you scout around for ideas, be sure to come up with some kind of filing system. Some writers mark large envelopes with various categories, and whenever they come across any material pertaining to those subjects, in it goes. But there is an easier way: Use an empty shoe box with a lid. Your notes and clippings are much more accessible that way. Whenever you see something you are sure you can use, just toss it into the box instead of filing it away. Later on, you can buy a small filing cabinet and organize your filler materials in a more orderly fashion. But when you are starting out, keep your filing system as simple as possible.

If you're sending your fillers to *Reader's Digest*, a magazine known for its readable nuggets of information, look before you leap—and crawl before you walk. Most of my students take it for granted that it's a breeze to get published in this magazine. I always have to remind them that there is stiff competition. Personal-experience pieces are difficult to do. To convince them, I have them choose an item from one of the magazines and write it down word for word. It doesn't take long for them to realize that there is a beginning, a middle and an end, and that the words seem to flow. They usually agree to try the small markets first, and then aim for the big one. You can benefit from this advice even if you are determined to send your materials to *Reader's Digest*. It will make your filler more polished, and give you a fighting chance to get accepted.

Manuscript Format

You are finally ready to mail out your little items—jokes, household hints, footnotes to history and personal experiences. Aside from the fact that they should be typed, what should they look like? What you are sending should look like this:

Henry M. Jones
236 Miller Lane   Appr. 120 words
Arlington, VA 22205

                        HUMOR IN UNIFORM

Every year on April Fool's Day, my thoughts go back to what happened to Sgt. Billings that morning.

But suppose there is no definite category for your item. Then what? In the following example, you are mailing in a recipe story to *Bon Appetit* magazine. Your best bet is to still do it this way:

Carol Jennings
5307 Kensington St   Appr. 220 words
Silver Spring, MD 33604

                        FOOD SECTION

One afternoon in 1830, Col. Robert Johnson stood on the steps of the courthouse in Salem, New Jersey, and performed a daring deed: He ate a tomato. Spectators were horrified and predicted he would be dead by morning.

Of course nothing happened, although through the centuries the idea has persisted that the succulent tomato . . .

Mailing and Marketing

A filler can be folded and placed in a long (No. 10) white envelope. Make sure that you keep a copy or save it on a computer disk. Unless specified otherwise, fillers will not be returned: If you haven't heard from the editor for sixty days, accept the fact that your item has been rejected. It's a good idea, when you are searching for markets, to list several of them in your little notebook. Then when it's time to "try, try again," your second choice is right there, and you won't have to scour your sources to find other publications.

If you make it a point to send out three or four fillers at about the same time, one rejection will not crush you. Later, when you are doing some articles and stories, always have two or three fillers out in the mail. They are easy to do, and will get accepted from time to time.

Read the list of markets for fillers in the September issue of *The Writer*. (You can find this magazine at the library or in a bookstore.) Get the feel of the target magazine or newspaper. Write down the name, address and the managing editor's name. If you can't get much information, write the words "Filler Market" on the outside of your envelope. Even that little touch will save the editors some wear and tear as they go through their daily avalanche of mail.

 Assignment

Write down some of the Christmas or Thanksgiving Day customs of your family.

5 NOW TRY A PERSONAL EXPERIENCE ARTICLE

Es war einmal ein junger Mann, and dieser Mann war Kadett an der amerikanischen Militarakadenie West Point.

(*German Catholic Digest*, 1957)

You have just read the first sentence of the first article I ever wrote. After arriving in Germany in the summer of 1956, I met the editor of the *German Catholic Digest* at a dinner. He asked me to write my impressions of his country and to describe the life of an army wife. I was flattered, of course, but I didn't know anything about article writing. In desperation, I started out by saying that once upon a time, there was a young man, a cadet at West Point, who met a young woman he really liked, and they decided to get married. From that time on, they lived in many parts of the United States and in Japan. I then went on and told about living in grandeur in some places and very simply in others. I discussed in detail what it was like to live on an army post, and described the setup of military quarters, the commissary, the post exchange, the clubs, the schools, the recreation facilities and so on. I eventually added my five children to the story and told about the hectic move to Aschaffenburg, Germany. Believe me, it was work! But as I wrote, I could see my stilted phrases turning into readable material. I even added some humor. I related the story of a friend of mine who, because of a flat tire, found herself stranded downtown. She called her husband and said she was on *Einbahnstrasse* near the bakery. When he roared with laughter, she knew she had done it again—a stranger in a strange land. *Einbahnstrasse* means "one-way street." (Even though I could speak the language fairly well, there were times when I too made faux pas.)

I'll always be grateful to those German editors who started me on my career in writing. In fact, they also bought my second article, "Meet My Friend, St. Jude," which had a much more polished lead.

It was inevitable, I suppose, that I write about my first German kaffeeklatsch. In the words of an old TV commercial, "I can't believe I ate the whole thing." I still can't believe it, and yet it was twenty-four years ago when I rang the bell of Frau Meyer's house and along with three other American wives stepped into the nineteenth century. A streamlined version of the article reads:

> The next time you "take ten" for a coffee break, give a thought to the American army wives stationed in Germany who are experiencing *der Grossvater von* all coffee breaks—a real *kaffeeklatsch*.
>
> American wives are always fascinated by the elaborate ritual of a German coffee party, and they find themselves accepting one invitation after another. But they soon discover, to their great horror, that the extra calories have an insidious way of turning into extra pounds, and they are soon fighting their own private Battle of the Bulge.
>
> I'll never forget my first *kaffeeklatsch* in the picture postcard town of Aschaffenburg. Why don't you come with me to 42 Gutwerk Strasse and meet our hostess? You'll see for yourself why this little social event is causing so many problems. . . . Elsa, Frau Meyer's maid, opens the door and

41

ushers us into an old-fashioned parlor. Frau Meyer comes forward to greet us and offers us some butter cookies and a glass of Rhine wine. (It's an afternoon affair.) After an hour of exchanging recipes and discussing topics ranging from politics to children, our hostess slides open the doors to her dining room. The table looks elegant with its Bavarian china and silver candlesticks; we can see that she went to great lengths to make us enjoy our visit.

And here comes Elsa with the first cake. It has a torte dough and is filled with pieces of fresh fruit covered by a gelatin glaze. Take some, but wait for the bowl of *Schlag* (whipped cream) to head your way. This is the real thing, with only a touch of sugar and vanilla added. One bit of advice—don't try to sneak only a smidgen onto your cake. Frau Meyer will look greatly dismayed and exclaim, "Oh, Mrs. Davis! You need more cream," and then she'll lean over and plop another blob onto your portion.

And just as you are finished, in comes the second cake.

It's a chocolate one made from a special recipe that comes from the Black Forest. You can't refuse: You're here to win brownie points for your country, remember? How about some you-know-what to put on top? Another cup of coffee? Don't look now, but here comes the bowl again.

What? You want to go home? Not yet. Our hostess leads us into a little sitting room, and here we must have a glass of apricot liqueur. Make sure you drink every shimmering drop laden with those double-barreled calories. Smile, woman, smile! And deep down inside you have to admit that everything you've had today has been delicious, delightful and delectable. You'll come back again—just like us.

In the spring of 1958, we found ourselves on the move again. This time it was to an exciting city 110 miles behind the Iron Curtain: Berlin! I knew I had to write about it—and I sold the story to *American Weekend* in record time. I called it "Quick, Ma, My Cloak and Dagger!" and described what it was like to move with five children into an area where there was an element of danger. I told about the train ride from Frankfurt, and about stopping at Marienburg so that the Russians could come aboard and check our passports, which took place in the middle of the night while everyone else was sound asleep. I peered out of the window, but rivers of rain on the glass made it almost impossible to see. This was the checkpoint, and from now on we would be in a Communist world until we reached Berlin. Part of the article read:

> As we raced on through the dismal night, I struggled to a sitting position from time to time and tried to catch glimpses of horror and intrigue in the countryside. Toward dawn, I gave up the fight because the rain beat so furiously at my window that I couldn't see a thing.
>
> The next morning at eight o'clock, we gathered our brood and baggage together and set foot in the lovely city of Berlin. We were escorted into an army sedan and whisked away to our German house in the American sector. . . . And so once again, for at least the thirtieth time in eighteen years, I settled down to the challenge of making a house into a home.
>
> (*American Weekend*, June 1958)

I went on to describe in Mata Hari style how I imagined seeing a spy behind every tree, or a Mercedes following me no matter where I went. I was doing it tongue-in-cheek, of course, but I found out later that I was closer to the truth than I'd realized.

As I wrote this article, I made a discovery. A style was beginning to emerge, one that sounded like me. It was helping me to sell my wares: The editors seemed to like it. When I look back on those days of teaching myself how to write, I know now that I was doing the right thing. The only way to learn to write is to write. The only way anyone can develop his own style is to put words to paper.

I was also learning how to write a tantalizing title and to sprinkle my material with anecdotes and quotes. But the next article I wrote was almost straight narrative because of the subject matter. It was my reaction to Premier Khrushchev's ultimatum of November 27, 1958. He called on the West to sign separate peace treaties with the Federal Republic and East Germany by May 27 of the following

43

year. If they refused to do so, Russia would sign a separate treaty with East Germany, and turn the supply lines to the city over to them. The ultimatum came at a time when the weather was cold, wet and gloomy, and I decided to tell the outside world how we felt behind the Iron Curtain. I never dreamed my article would hit the front page of *American Weekend* and be read throughout Europe. My lead did the trick.

> Frankly, I don't know how much longer I can stand being in the dark. Even though it has only been a matter of ten days since it all began, it seems as though an eternity has gone by. . . . Even this old house has lost its charm because there is no longer any laughter echoing throughout its rooms. An air of gloom has settled over all of us, and everyone goes silently about their tasks, wondering if there will be further complications.
>
> Oh, wait a minute! Do you think I'm talking about the situation here in Berlin? Oh, no! I'm just describing what it's like to have two small boys sick with the measles.
>
> (*American Weekend*, December 1958)

My children did have a bad case of this childhood disease and caused us a great deal of worry. The rest of the article did bring out the fact that the American families were so caught up in everyday living and coping with an epidemic of flu that they had little time to be concerned about world affairs. A few weeks later, I met our commanding general at a party and breathed a sigh of relief when he stared at me—and grinned.

Were all of my articles written overseas? It seems that way, but I have done a number of them much closer to home. You have heard many times, "Write about the things you know." It doesn't really matter where you are. Now is the time for you to jot down notes on events in your life that will be of interest to other people.

My Students and Their Experiences

Think back. Can you recall an adventure of your own? Have you seen a ghost or a flying saucer? Had an out-of-body experience?

44

Gone on a safari in Africa? Traveled through the Bermuda Triangle? Taken a cruise around the world? Visited the Taj Mahal? Owned a remarkable pet? Interviewed a celebrity? My students have written about these items—and have gotten published!

If you have lived through a traumatic experience, you may wish to write it up for a religious magazine; one of my students did just that and sent her article to *Seek*, an Adult Sunday School publication. She not only wrote about what it was like to go through this experience, but also told about the power of prayer and how that helped. She sold it. (This was her first sale.)

The only time I slanted an article toward a religious magazine was years ago when my children were small and I was putting them through the third degree to find out who had cut off the cat's whiskers. What made the deed even more dastardly was the fact that only the right side of Tiger's face had been tampered with, making her look particularly ridiculous. What I had in mind was to write something about mothers and how they must face life with courage and fortitude and patience. But I knew that I needed a peg on which to hang my tale of woe. And it materialized when I attended a church service for mothers only a few Sundays later.

The young Irish priest who was the guest speaker told us that we were already on the way to sainthood. His four married sisters and their myriads of children always made him content with his life whenever he paid them a visit. Raising offspring requires heroic qualities, the good Father said. And he admitted that he always breathed a sigh of relief whenever he left his nephews and nieces. I laughed along with the other women, but as I drove home, I mulled over what he had told us. Why couldn't I become a saint? I decided to give myself a trial run for one whole week.

Monday was uneventful. On Tuesday, I almost picked up the phone to tell Alice what I had heard about Betty. On Wednesday, the car stalled downtown, and I swallowed the words I wanted to say. On Thursday, I tripped over Tinker Toys and choked on an expression or two tucked away in my subconscious. On Friday, I began to grumble as I groped under beds for socks and missing items. On Saturday, I smiled a lot. But on Sunday, the dam broke. I was getting ready to go to a formal reception and couldn't find my new pink lipstick. My five-year-old was watching me as I scurried about and bemoaned my loss. Then, in a calm voice, he said, "It's over there on the windowsill." I ran into the bathroom, grabbed it, applied it—and heard him add, "It fell into the toilet bowl, but I got it out." I froze. But my sense of humor took over and I laughed until I cried. I wrote up my story and sent it to *Ave Maria*, a national publication. Several months later, there it was on the front page of the magazine. Underneath the title "The Time I Almost Became a Saint" was a sketch of a halo a little askew. Later it was also picked up by *Family Digest*.

What would you do if you were given a million dollars? A local retired real estate investor and millionaire recently sponsored an essay contest and was impressed with the answers he received. Milan Herman, one of my students, placed third among 1,300 contributors. The first prize of $1,000 was won by a man who said he would set up a fund for catastrophic situations that couldn't be handled by today's organizations. Milan wrote about developing self-esteem, and said that she would use the money to attack negative thinking. She fully believes "Man is what he thinks; he can go forward only if he first has a desire for a better life." She used several quotes from Napoleon Hill and W. Clement Stone, whose books have inspired thousands to reach their full potential. Milan didn't receive any money, but this was her first success in the writing field, and she now plans to do articles on a course she is taking on Alpha mind power. (There is a footnote to this story: The man who sponsored the contest announced that he is going to establish a foundation for catastrophic situations.) If you find yourself wishing that you had the opportunity to win a touch of fame or fortune, look around you—and read your daily newspaper with the eyes of a hawk. Pounce on any item that gives you a chance to use your way with words so you can gain the experience you need to become a professional writer.

For other personal article ideas, you can write about health news or sports activities such as boating, golf, hunting, fishing and martial arts. What's "hot" right now are personal articles on sky-diving, surfing and scuba-diving.

Article Structure

If your thoughts have been racing as you read this information, you must be asking yourself how to begin. There is a kind of formula to article writing: If you master it, you will be able to turn out salable material ranging from a 600-word feature to a 2,500-word detailed piece of nonfiction. Every article needs the following:

1. A provocative title
2. A narrative hook or lead
3. An anecdote or a quote (one or more), or dialogue
4. Good transitional sentences
5. A summary ending

Choose the right title and you'll have an editor grabbing your manuscript the minute he sees it. Here are some of mine:

- "Maid in Japan," which told about the wonderful woman who worked for us in the Land of the Rising Sun.
- "The Things I've Swallowed for My Country," which described the various foods I've eaten in foreign countries.
- "The Year I Saw Stars," which revolved around the famous men and women I interviewed on a radio program.
- "Would I Do It Again?" which gave a rundown of my life as an army wife and stated that I would do it all over again if I had the chance.

I've become a title freak and collect them whenever I can. For example, a local TV station presents its weekly monster movie under the title "Creature Feature." A secondhand dress shop not far from here calls itself "The Second Time Around," and a new one close by is known as "Once Is Not Enough." A current book on genealogy by Suzanne Hilton is called *Who Do You Think You Are?* When I started teaching writing fifteen years ago, I decided to call the course "Write Now!" and I honestly believe that the title motivated a number of people to sign up. If you find that you're having trouble coming up with a title, try creating one with alliteration. Two or three words that begin with the same letter sound pleasant to the inner ear: *The Wind in the Willows, Loon Lake* and *Little Lord Fauntleroy* are good examples of this kind of heading.

Of all the aspects involved in writing an article, the most important is the narrative hook. It should "hook" the reader into wanting to read on and enjoy or learn from the item. You will have to experiment and find out which lead suits you best. There are five I especially recommend.

1. **The anecdote.** This one will tell a little story.

   Tom Bingham discovered the secret in the attic one rainy morning when he awoke before his wife and had little to do. He decided to investigate a loose spot of wallpaper where he had become convinced that a mysterious secret door lay hidden.

2. **The comparison.** This one usually compares two things.

   While the search is on again for the Abominable Snowman, there is another species of the human race that deserves attention. She is known as the Army Wife.

3. **The question.** This lead should be provocative.

   Did you know that sixty thousand wives ran away from home last year?

4. **A quote.** This lead can come from a famous person or an authority on the subject you're writing about.

5. **A startling fact.** This narrative hook should make the reader sit up and take notice.

   If you should visit the British Museum in London one of these days, you would, no doubt, be impressed with the mummified body of an Egyptian woman more than five thousand years old. But what would really make an impact is the fact that her fingernails are painted a dark red.

When you have chosen your lead, you are ready for your second paragraph. It should set the scene and give the reader an idea what the article is all about. The end of the article should be a summary of what you have been saying. If you find yourself floundering and becoming long-winded at this point, take a look at your second paragraph and "Play it again, Sam," but use different words. Make it short and sweet; don't let your endings drag on and on.

And what comes in between? If your article is short, you can get by with one quote or anecdote. But if it is more than 1,200 words, sprinkle it with several. These little touches add backbone and authority to your material. Suppose you are writing about goals in life and how important they are. You could use a quote from Abraham Lincoln: "I will study and prepare myself, and then, someday, my chance will come." Or you could use a line from Shakespeare: "What's brave, what's noble, let's do it!"

If your article is more than 1,500 words, it is a good idea to send a query letter to an editor. Put your best foot forward by catching his attention at the beginning with an intriguing item from your manuscript. Make sure you send a self-addressed stamped envelope (SASE)—and don't be surprised to get a go-ahead from the publication you're aiming for. (If this kind of letter writing is causing a furrow in your brow, take heart. There is a sample in the next chapter.)

In 1989, a retiree in one of my classes was thrilled to have the following article accepted by the *Washington Post*:

Little Schoolhouse on the Prairie
BY ORLIN SCOVILLE

My school stood on a bluff rising from Bijou Creek, seven miles west of Fort Morgan, Colorado. The plain white structure was in the midst of corn and sorghum fields and prairies. You could see it for miles around. It was officially known as District 3, School No. 5, but we just called it Bijou Hill School.

The school had one room and a cloakroom, a well and hand-pump, a flag pole, two privies and a shed for the horses. The school was intended to be a community center as well, so it was equipped with kerosene lamps perched on brackets along the walls. There was a big round stove—a coal-burning Round Oak—in the middle of the room.

My brother and I walked the half-mile or so morning and evening, carrying our lunches in shiny round lard pails. The children who lived a couple of miles away rode a horse or drove a buggy.

At school we sat in rows according to grade, and the desks got bigger, row by row. We could measure our physical and academic progress as we advanced each fall toward the right side of the room. All, that is, except poor Ormey, whose body grew but whose mind did not. So he stayed at the left row of desks until he virtually had to be stuffed into his seat.

There was a bench at the front for each class, in turn, to use while reciting. Most years, we had one or two pupils in each grade, so the teacher was kept busy. It was a studious atmosphere. When not reciting, you were preparing a lesson or reading, and keeping still was important. The teacher usually had a foot-long ruler, with which you would get a thwack on the forearm if you were bad. Little kids were paddled by hand. Alternatively, you could be kept in at recess and made to do sums or, if small, practice writing your alphabet.

For a library, we had a row of shelves containing the *Book of Knowledge*, a dictionary, a few reference books and a few dog-eared texts. The county had a traveling library that brought books around every month or so, packaged in what appeared to be one unit of a sectional bookcase with handles on either end.

With its mixture of children of all sizes, the school was like a large family, with little kids riding on the shoulders of big kids, for whom they had great respect, trust and loyalty. In my first year it was suggested by one of my big buddies that I should kiss fellow first-grader BeeDee Hamilton, and so I did. My friends then turned on me, each pointing a finger and scraping the forefinger of the other hand across it in the traditional "For Shame" sign. I was crushed and bawled like a calf, so they put me on their shoulders again to restore my spirit.

We behaved as a family in many other ways. We shared messages from brothers and uncles who were serving with the AEF in France. We passed around the whooping cough and measles, few of us having been vaccinated. As a second-grader, I shared the fear of the influenza epidemic of 1918, although, mercifully, it touched none of us. Several of us wore little bags of asafetida around our necks, as recommended by contemporary folk wisdom.

At recess and lunchtime we played games: Tag, Hide-and-Seek and Anti-Over—throwing a ball over the roof to be caught by someone and thrown back. Fox and Geese was played in the winter, when the required wheel-and-spoke playing field could be marked out in the snow (the hub was safe territory for the geese).

Baseball was adapted to the number of players available. The usual game was "Work-Up." The whole team would be deployed on the field. When the batter was put out, he went to a fielder position, the pitcher became batter, the catcher became pitcher and so on, each one advancing one position. Winners were the batters who got the most runs. Shinney, a variation of field hockey, was played with a hockey stick made from a discarded board, and a battered tin can was the puck.

There were also games for two players, like mumblety-peg, played with a jackknife, the blade fully open and the small blade on the same end half-open. You flipped the knife and scored the most points if the big blade stuck upright in the ground. If the knife was a "leaner," with both big and little blades in the ground, you got half as many points.

Playground games were democratic, with team captains chosen for seniority and skill. The captains "chose-up" their teams regardless of sex: How well you played was all that mattered. Our handicapped boy joined us in the games he understood.

My teachers were a varied lot. In my first year we had Willard Graham, a practice teacher from the high school. He rode in on his Harley Davidson motorcycle every morning. We thought he was great. The next year we had Miss Perry, a backwoods teacher from the South who put gravy on her oatmeal and completely mixed us up into groups that didn't make sense—I think we were arrayed by height. The parents rose in anger at the school superintendent, and she was sent somewhere else. Her place was taken by the wife of a neighboring farmer, who was well trained and had taught in the Denver schools before she married. She was a good teacher.

By the seventh grade, I had no classmates. The teacher thought I was becoming bored, so I skipped a grade.

We had various celebrations and festivities at school. Christmas was a big occasion. A parent would bring in a tree from the mountains 100 miles away, and we would spend weeks preparing the trimmings: paper chains and popcorn strings. Real candles were put in metal holders and clipped to the tree. It was a beautiful sight when lighted, but it is a miracle we weren't incinerated. Families brought gifts for the children and parked them under the tree. Carols were sung and children spoke their pieces. There was the sound of sleigh bells in the yard, and Santa came in to hand out the gifts.

On Sunday, our school was the gathering place for a community Sunday School attended by folk of all ages and many persuasions.

Occasionally, a community group would put on a box social, mostly for the benefit of the young single people. The main event was the auctioning of boxes, prepared by the ladies and containing a meal for two. The lucky fellow buying the box got to eat with the lady who had prepared it.

At the end of the school year, there was a picnic beside the Platte River. Deep enough for wading but not swimming, the Platte has been referred to as being "a mile wide, but so shallow a fish has to stand on his head to keep his gills wet." The old folks sat in the shade and talked about the crops and the old times, while the children, properly warned about quicksand, explored the cottonwoods and the willow thickets, and tried to catch minnows in shallow pools.

From Bijou Hill, I went to the city high school and then to Colorado Agricultural College, where my grammatical skills were examined and found to be nonexistent. I was forthwith required to take "Boob English." Aside from that indignity, I seem to have suffered no ill effects from having gone to a country school.

In my years at Bijou Hill School, I must have known about twenty fellow-pupils. Most of us went on to high school and then became farmers, artisans, office workers and homemakers, all worthy occupations. Three got Ph.D.s from prestigious universities and became college professors. One went to West Point and retired a colonel.

The one-room school was a treasured experience shared by many boys and girls in the early years of this century. There were 200,100 single-teacher schools when the government first counted them in 1915–1916. By 1986–1987, the number had dropped to 772, making one-room-school teachers an endangered species indeed. In our little schools there was peer-group teaching and learning and self-discovery, now called "heuristic learning" by the pedagogues. The teacher, who had us almost one-on-one in little groups, was the key to the process. She would come to know our idiosyncrasies and strengths over the years. Even handicapped Ormey had the privilege of being "mainstreamed," to use the jargon of progressive educators.

It has been said that "The Battle of Waterloo was won on the playing fields of Eton." The products of one-room schools may have won no great military victories, but the lessons learned there—of teamwork, initiative, self-reliance and making do with very little—helped us fight our way through the Great Depression, the Waterloo of our generation.

 *Assignment*

Now is the time to write about the flying saucer you saw one starry night outside your bedroom window. Send the article to *Fate* magazine (listed in *Writer's Market).*

6 HOW ABOUT A RESEARCH ARTICLE?

A number of years ago, the phone rang and an editor of the *Army Times* said, "How would you like to do an article on tipping for our upcoming travel supplement?" I paused—and then agreed before I could think.

Later, as I did some routine things around the house, I muttered to myself as it dawned on me that what I knew about tipping could be said in one sentence: Waiters expect 15 percent of the bill, and hairdressers about the same. How could I ever put together 1,500 words for Ruth? The answer, of course, was to ask my traveling friends and do some research.

But when I checked with the people I knew who seemed to be always flitting from coast to coast, they were surprisingly vague. They finally admitted that most of the time they overtipped because they didn't know how much to give. There certainly is a need for this kind of article, I thought. And once again I was impressed with editors and their uncanny knack for knowing what the public needs.

The next day, I trekked down to the library and tried to find details on tipping. The librarian tried to help, but couldn't come up with anything until she looked at the compact edition of the *Oxford English Dictionary*. Its two volumes contain all the words one would find in the original thirteen volumes, printed in microscopic type. It comes with a magnifying glass. No matter how I tried to read it, I couldn't do it. I then picked up a Fodor book on travel and checked it out for a few days. It helped, but not much.

One of the women in my writing class saved the day. She came in with a recent issue of *Travel & Leisure*, and in it appeared tipping do's and don'ts for the United States. It was just what I needed. But there was one more thing I had to unearth: How did the custom of tipping get started?

I called the reference librarian at the main library and she managed to find the answer in a book called *A Book About a Thousand Things*, by George Stimpson. I trudged down to Central to read the material for myself, and could hardly put the book down. But I jotted down the details and dashed out the door, eager to get started on a challenging writing project.

That spring, my article, "Timely Tips on Tipping," appeared. Part of it looked like this:

> Your bags are packed. Tour travel arrangements have been checked and rechecked and you're rarin' to go. But once again a cloud on the horizon threatens to spoil your trip: How much should you tip, and who should receive the gratuity?
>
> Relax. Stop muttering, and accept the fact that the quaint old custom of tipping is here to stay. And it is old and quaint. According to historians, it all started three centuries ago in London.
>
> The story is told that it was customary in those days to have boxes in English inns and coffee houses for the receipt of coins for the benefit of waiters. "To Insure Promptness" was printed on the boxes to remind guests of the way to get special service. Sometimes the phrase was abbreviated to T.I.P. To this day, the British don't realize what a Pandora's box they created so innocently in the seventeenth century.
>
> (*Army Times,* May 1980)

The rest of the article was done alphabetically, starting with "Airlines" and ending with "Trains." I saved a special tidbit for my ending (many writers use this device).

And after reading all of these details on tipping, you may be tempted to sign up for the first space shuttle flight to another planet. You won't have to travel that far. You can plan a trip to China, where tipping is unacceptable—and even considered rude.

Several of my students did quite well when they ventured out into the research field. Lila Parker, a retired government worker, wrote a short article on tea. She had an intriguing first paragraph pointing out that tea is a mystical, delightful brew with special powers and stating that its magic has been believed in and sought for ages.

She then went on and described the different kinds of tea, going back to ancient times, and ended with

I pray that, risen from the dead,
I may in Glory stand;
A crown, perhaps, upon my head
But a teacup in my hand.

The article was published in a weekly newspaper.

Nan Carroll, a history buff, wrote an article on our Declaration of Independence. Did you know that it was hidden in many places after it was signed? Whenever war threatened, it was moved to a safe place, including a linen sack in a barn in 1814 and in a vault at Fort Knox in 1941. Her story was published in a regional magazine.

Another student wrote about the osprey, a huge bird she would see on her weekly trips to the Eastern Shore in Maryland. She queried the editor of the *Baltimore Sun* about doing an article, he said yes, and it was published, too. He told her that these birds were a sign of spring, and her timing was right on the money for his paper coming out at the end of March.

My own research often led me into the history field. One article I'll never forget was accepted by a TV magazine published by a station in California. It featured the life of Elizabeth I and served as an introduction, or lead in, to a TV series on her life—I'll never try anything like that again. I read so many books on the Virgin Queen that I'll be an authority on her for years to come. The whole subject was too much to cover.

In doing an article, especially in the research field, you will have to learn how to weave in interesting facts and still keep the momentum going. When you look over your pages of material, one of those facts could give you a title, and maybe a great narrative hook or lead.

In a recent issue of *Astronomy* magazine, Ron Cowen, a science writer, did a fascinating article on the dinosaurs. His title? "The Day the Dinosaurs Died." But his short introduction was even better. It said:

> For more than four billion years, it orbits the sun—a pock-marked, misshapen body roughly the size of Manhattan. Over time, it wandered into the inner solar system, occasionally passing near our planet as it journeyed around the Sun. Then one day about sixty-five million years ago, Earth and the rough-hewn body reached the same place at exactly the same time.

Can this happen again? Arthur C. Clarke, the famous writer and scientist, says it can—and will.

When you write your research article, take a look at the magazines in your library or in *Writer's Market*. Jot down names of magazines that could be interested in your kind of articles. Send a query letter or two—or three. Don't write the article until you get a favorable response. Then, when you know what the editor wants, write your article—maybe with a slant from the editor himself, one you hadn't thought of.

Here are more article ideas that require research.

- Did Atlantis exist?
- Was there a King Arthur?
- Can trees communicate with each other?
- There are nine new planets out there and Mars shows signs of primitive life: How would you feel if we discover that we are not alone? (This could be a personal article for a religious magazine.)

- Who are the three ghosts living in the White House?
- Is it true that by the year 2000 we could fly around the world in eighty hours?
- Would you live on the moon or Mars if we colonize there?
- What is the Holy Grail?
- What are some of the changes coming in the twenty-first century?

Here are some other ideas for research that should prove fun to do *and* challenging.

- The Titanic has finally been found. According to reliable reports, the original copy of *The Rubáiyát of Omar Khayyám* was on board. Why? Where was it going? Who had bought it?
- King Arthur is alive and well and living in Cornwall, England—or so legend says. He will come to his country's rescue whenever he is needed. Was there ever a King Arthur or a Merlin?
- What are the ten books that changed the world?
- What grows between the roots of pine, oak or willow trees? The truffle, of course. What is a truffle? Did you know that truffles can be found in California around Santa Rosa?
- Is Noah's Ark on Mount Ararat? What do the aerial photos show? What is the latest word from the expedition?
- Did you know that shoes were so important in the early life of man that they were given magical powers—and that they once were used as money and food?
- Did you know that there is a phantom ship that sails the Hudson River? Is it the *Flying Dutchman* finding a port at last, Henry Hudson's *Half Moon* looking for its captain, or Captain Kidd coming back for his treasure?
- Have you heard of the Chalice of Nanteos in Wales? It is supposed to be the cup used by Christ at the Last Supper. It has been on exhibit at Nanteos House every summer for many years, and people from all over the world have come to see it. But a short time ago, the woman who owned the house and chalice simply vanished. What happened? And where is the fragile, olive-wood bowl today?

58

- How would you like to take a college course, talk to a friend and visit your doctor—without leaving your living room? It's happening now through communications satellites.
- Christopher Columbus discovered America, but he also came across the pineapple, the green turtle and what other foods?
- Why are there blue-eyed Indians in the Carolinas? Could they be descendants of the "Lost Colony?"
- Did you know that popcorn was the first "puffed" breakfast cereal eaten by our early settlers? And that the Iroquois made popcorn soup?
- What is folklore? How much of it is true?
- Have you ever heard of the Baker Street Irregulars? Who are they?
- Are you an authority on roses? In addition to telling amateurs to plant them as early as possible in the spring, why don't you also inform them that fossilized rose petals 35 million years old have been found in Oregon and Montana; George Washington was our first rose breeder; and James Brady, a White House gardener, developed the American Beauty during Grant's administration.
- Why do Canadians feed their cats very well on Christmas Eve? What special event takes place in Germany on December 6? Who created the first creche?
- Do you suffer from Ozmania? Many people do, and they enjoy every minute of it: They are admirers of L. Frank Baum, who wrote the fourteen Oz books, and every year they flock to the convention held in Castle Park, Michigan. Who was this man? How did he become such a storyteller?

Time to Begin

Now that you have some subject matter to research and write about, what should be your next move? Since you are a beginning writer, choose a topic in which you have some expertise or interest. After you choose your idea, jot down some important points and develop them into a blueprint or outline. This preliminary work will also help you write a more convincing query letter later on.

(Make sure that your query is well thought out, and not just a half-baked idea.)

Now begin to fill in this framework from your knowledge, and then browse through your encyclopedias for more information. But don't stop here. Go to the library and see what new books and articles have been written on your subject. This is also the time to check *Books in Print* in case there are publications on the subject not available at your library. The *Reader's Guide to Periodical Literature* will tell you what articles have been written about your topic. If there is an expert in the field living in your area, set up an interview with her. Later, add these bits of new information to what you have on hand. And now comes a very important part of article writing: Read through what you have written or typed, ferret out an intriguing item and use it for the lead in your query letter.

Let's suppose you have decided to write about the VIP ghosts at 1600 Pennsylvania Avenue, Washington, DC. You live nearby and plan to contact Lillian Parks, who co-authored *My Thirty Years Backstairs at the White House*. What publications should you aim for? Why not try a new magazine for children called *Cobblestone*, and mention to the editor that it would make a different Halloween story for their October issue? If you have this in mind, remember that you should send seasonal material at least six months ahead of time for magazines, and about five weeks for newspapers. This means that your query must go out several weeks before those deadlines.

The Query Letter

And now, at last, you're ready to write that letter. First of all, find out the name of the current editor of the magazine or newspaper to whom you plan to send your article. You can do this in several ways. Look at the publication's masthead, which lists the names of the staff members. Try to find the article's editor, if possible. If you have trouble finding the person who is in charge of the section you're aiming for, call and ask the personnel office. You can also go through a current copy of the *Writer's Digest* or *The Writer* and look through the article markets written up in detail. Each one will contain the name of the editor and what she is looking for. *Writer's Market*, an annual directory, is a good source for editors' names in the article field, but you may want to check the magazines for possible updates. If all else fails, and you can't find out the name of the person in charge, simply say "Dear Editor."

Type your query single-spaced, and have it cover about a page. Do your usual heading and then say:

Dear Editor:

Did you know that the White House has ghosts? Don't visualize run-of-the-mill spirits, however; these are VIPs who have played an important role in history. What is especially amazing is the fact that they have been seen by down-to-earth, reliable people.

Would you like to see a 1,500-word article about the ghosts of Abraham Lincoln, Dolly Madison and Abigail Adams and where they make their appearances? I plan to describe what happened when they were seen, and why the rumor is growing that our President's home is definitely haunted.

In the course of my research, I have been in contact with Lillian Parks, the co-author of *My Thirty Years Backstairs at the White House*. She is providing me with some details that will add a special touch to my story.

I'm an elementary school teacher who knows that young people are always intrigued by ghosts in any shape or form. Frankly, so am I!

Sincerely,

As your credits grow, you can mention toward the end of your letter the fact that you have sold some articles or stories. It's a good idea to state that you have studied the format of the publication. You should do this in every category of writing. If you become familiar with the magazine or newspaper, you'll know if your style of writing fits in with the editor's needs.

Send out your query with a self-addressed stamped envelope. You should receive an answer in two or three weeks. If it's positive, whip your article into shape. Make sure you have a tantalizing title, a narrative hook bound to whet the appetite of your reader, a second paragraph that sets the scene, a sprinkling of anecdotes, quotes or dialogue and a summary ending or one that adds a special zing to your subject.

Fold your manuscript, put it into a white No. 10 envelope and make sure you enclose a SASE. If your article is more than five pages, it is a wise idea to place it in a folder and then mail it out in a 10 × 13 envelope. Always keep a copy and record the mailing date. When two months have gone by, send a polite note to the editor to find out what happened to your submission.

If photography is your hobby, get into the habit of mailing 5 × 7 black-and-white glossies with your manuscript. You'll be able to sell to some of the slick magazines and make more money. If you don't know one end of the camera from the other, you can obtain pictures free, or for a nominal sum, from public relations departments, government offices, the Library of Congress and the National Archives. Other sources are listed in *The Writer's Ultimate Research Guide,* published by Writer's Digest Books. (This book is a boon to all article writers because it lists all kinds of subjects.) Remember, however, that you will be able to sell your material without photographs: I've been doing it for many years.

A footnote: The moment your manuscript has hit the sack at the post office, get those mental wheels turning again and come up with another idea to work on. Don't sit and wait for word from the editor. A professional writer goes on to bigger and better things immediately.

 Assignment

Choose an article idea, look up the subject in your encyclopedia and then get a book or two on it from your library. Jot down facts. Eventually, when you read your notes over and over, you'll see a title and a terrific lead. (Be sure to take a look at chapter five to see how an article is structured.)

7 THE JUVENILE SCENE: FICTION, NONFICTION AND POETRY

Selling My First Juvenile Story

It may sound strange, but one of the best things that ever happened to me in my writing career involved a rejection slip. It took place years ago when my family and I returned from a two-year stint in Kyoto, Japan. I had soaked up so many fascinating facts about Japan that I had to tell Americans all about it. I decided to write a children's story, something I hadn't done before.

I described the life of a nine-year-old boy named Yozo, and told about his lifestyle, which included eating his meals at a low table, eating with chopsticks, sleeping on a futon (a thick quilt) instead of a bed and having a cricket for a pet. The story line was about Yozo going to the American School to perform a violin solo one morning and how excited he was. The words seemed to flow, and I quickly sent it off to a well-known national magazine called *Children's Activities*.

It came back in just a few days. I couldn't believe it! But there was a note from the editor, who said, "Interesting material, but this is not a story. Give Yozo a problem!" I did, sent it to her again and sold it. I'll always be grateful to this woman who gave me a valuable lesson in writing fiction.

When I rewrote it, I wove many of the customs into the fabric of the story—which should be done so that the material doesn't sound like a article. Here are some lines:

> Yozo seemed to hear a voice calling him from far away. He slowly opened his eyes, and there stood his mother with his new clothes over her arm.
>
> "Wake up, Yozo! Wake up!" she was saying.
>
> Yozo thought a second. Then he jumped up from his bed on the floor.
>
> "Today is the day! Today is the day!" he cried. "Are those my new clothes? Where is my breakfast?"
>
> "Not so fast, my young son. Go put your futon in the closet the way you do every morning. There is still time for that."
>
> Yozo folded his quilt and went over to the closet. He pushed open the sliding door, put the quilt inside and closed the door. Now the bedroom had become the living room once again.

During the next ten years I wrote several children's stories, but from time to time I went back to doing articles. I found them easier to do. If you have always wanted to write stories for children, however, plunge in by beating a path to your library. Talk to the librarian, and ask her what is being read now. The picture changes from time to time. Many editors are no longer looking for stories about divorce, drugs or dysfunctional families, or tales of horror. Now is the time to write that fantasy book, or to tell about the gentle dragon that lives in your son's imagination.

The Age Groups

While these thoughts are swirling around in your head, decide which age group you'd like to write for. There are five to choose from:

- Three to six: the picture-book crowd
- Six to eight: the beginning reader
- Eight to twelve: the easiest age group to write for

- Twelve to fifteen: the most difficult group
- The reluctant reader: fairly new, and includes every age

The Picture-Book Crowd

If you would like to write for the three-to-six age group, be aware that your story or text must complement the pictures. Your manuscript supplies half of the book; the artist does the rest. Also take into consideration that young readers have a short attention span. Don't get bogged down with detail: Keep your sentences short and your words simple. And once again, start your story with an intriguing tidbit that will make that little boy or girl eager to turn the page.

What should you write about? Tell a story about a cowboy, a clown, a rabbit, a dog, a kitten, a caterpillar, a horse, a cow, a chicken, a bear, a kangaroo or a witch. They have all been used in books during the past few years and have earned a spot on the library shelf. You could even do a simple mystery. Right now there is a preschooler book at my library called *The Mystery of the Red Mitten*, by Steven Kellogg. It is aimed toward the two-year-old child. Books for that tender age are now finding their way into the juvenile section.

The ingenuity of the writers for this age group amazes me. Recently, they came up with the idea of using the "scratch-and-sniff" technique (invented by advertisers) in a number of books. Have you seen-and-sniffed the one about the smells of Christmas? The author made sure to include the wonderful fragrances of pine, gingerbread and candy canes. Another one I enjoyed was a mystery that could only be solved only by sniffing the clues on each page.

If you want to try a picture book some day, make sure to use repetition in your story. Young children like to read words or phrases over and over again. Reread your battered copy of *The Wind in the Willows* by Kenneth Grahame. Read it aloud, and enjoy such lines as "So he scraped and scratched and scrabbled and scrooged and then he scrooged again and scrabbled and scratched and scraped." A word of caution: Writing for this age group looks easy, but the men and women who create these books admit they work on each one for a long, long time. They suggest that anyone entering this field spend many hours at the library.

Has Dr. Seuss always been one of your favorite authors? His early attempts at writing should encourage you to try, try again if your book ideas are turned down at first. His first manuscript, *And to Think That I Saw It on Mulberry Street,* was rejected by twenty publishers before his big break came. Theodor Geisel (Dr. Seuss's real name) says that he was planning to burn his manuscript when he happened to run into an old college friend he hadn't seen for some time. He was surprised when he learned that his friend was now the children's book editor for Vanguard Press. Geisel mentioned the story he had written, showed it to the interested editor— and Dr. Seuss was born. Since that time, his books have sold eighty million copies in this country alone, and he has won international fame with his Loraxes, Drum-Tummied Snumms and Grinches.

Beginning Readers

If you're interested in doing a book for the six-to-eight age group, you're hitting a mushrooming market. The next time you go to the library, look for the "beginning reader" section and take some books home. You'll find material on science, famous people, American history, animals and even grammar, all written in a way that appeals to the young reader. And, of course, you'll also come across books of adventure, mystery and everyday happenings that capture the imagination of youngsters learning to read.

A mystery that has done well in this age category is *The Secret Three,* by Mildred Myrick (Harper & Row, 1964). It is still popular, and I know why. It revolves around secret codes, messages in bottles and three boys who form a secret club. Mildred joined one of my writing classes not too long ago, and is now working on a story about a boy ghost who doesn't want to wear white. I asked her where she found the ideas for her successful story, and she told me that during the years she had been a librarian, she observed what books appealed to boys who were six, seven and eight.

Before attempting to do this kind of story, it is important that you become familiar with the format. There are only a few words to each line, so that the beginning reader is not intimidated in any way. Here is a passage from *The Secret Three.*

Mark came to stay with Billy
at the beach.
"Let's go for a swim,"
said Mark.
"We have to wait an hour
after we eat," said Billy.
"Let's take a walk on the beach.
The tide was high this morning.
We may find something good
on the sand."

The Preteen Group

If you're planning to try the eight-to-twelve age group, you'll be working in the category that is the easiest to do. The majority of the books in the children's section at your library are for this age span. They cover all kinds of subjects: sports, school, mystery, adventure, fantasy, legends, ghosts tales, life in foreign lands, folk tales and family living. But other topics are finding their way into this age level, and you'll find books on divorce, ethnic problems and other social issues. If you lean more toward realistic fiction, read the books written by Judy Blume, who has achieved great success in this field. But no matter which direction you go, make sure that your protagonist is a year or two older than the age level you're writing for. This holds true for all of the age groups I've mentioned except the little picture-book people.

The Twelve-to-Fifteen Year Olds

In the early-teens age group, girls are interested in mysteries, career stories and light romances, including boy-girl relationships at school. Boys seem to prefer sports, outdoor adventure, mysteries and space, including science fiction. There is a dearth of material for these readers. The eight-to-twelve age group is easier to please because of their burgeoning curiosity, but young teenagers are in the midst of finding their own identity, and their reading tastes change from day to day.

Do you remember what you were reading at this stage in your life when you were neither fish nor fowl? If Nancy Drew or the

Hardy Boys pop into your mind, you'll be happy to hear that they are still being read today. They seem to be an integral part of growing up, even though they are not literary masterpieces. Harriet Stratemeyer Adams, an author for both series, managed to turn out a new Nancy Drew every year.

Reluctant Readers

Writing for the reluctant reader is another trend in children's fiction that is gaining momentum. These "hi-low" books are a challenge to write because they must intrigue the reader at once, but contain a limited vocabulary. During the past four years, I have written stories about Nathan Hale, Christopher Columbus, Jules Verne, Mary Shelley and Robert Louis Stevenson using this "hi-low" approach, and have sold them to an educational publisher who is interested in the reluctant reader. When I wrote my two-page sketches of these famous men and women, I knew I would have to reach out and grab my reader before he realized what had happened. Here are three of my narrative hooks.

Mary Shelley jumped up in bed, her eyes filled with terror. She had just seen a manlike monster brought to life! Was it real? Was she dreaming? She looked over at her husband, who was sound asleep, and felt better. There was nothing to worry about. But when she finally dozed off, the ghastly figure came back again!

When Robert Louis Stevenson was forty-one years old, he did a very strange thing: He gave away his birthday.

Step into your time machine and travel back to the fifteenth century. You are on a small sailing vessel in the middle of the Sea of Darkness. This sea is really part of the great Atlantic Ocean. No one has ever been here before Columbus.

These stories were a combination of fact and fiction, but were based on thorough research. I had to be careful not to stretch my imagination beyond a certain point, or I would be distorting history or the life of a well-known figure.

Instead of writing for young children, you may wish to try the young adult field for the twelve-to-fifteen age group. These books are usually paperbacks, and your best bet is to go to your library or bookstore and pick up a few to read. Most of them run 40,000 words, and many of the editors want to see the first three chapters and a synopsis instead of the whole manuscript. Most of them are mysteries or love stories, and will pay you about $2,000 if accepted.

Nonfiction

If you are interested in writing nonfiction for children and young adults, try your hand at doing a biography. Choose a man or woman that you admire. Take a look at the biographies done by Jean Fritz more than twenty years ago. With delightful titles such as *Where Do You Think You Are Going, Columbus?* and *And Then What Happened, Paul Revere?*, they are still popular today. Mrs. Fritz writes with humor, but her facts are always accurate. She is an excellent researcher. The biographies you'll see in the juvenile section at your library are not only in the history field. Biographies are now being written about sports figures, celebrities, men and women in space, explorers—and even Jules Verne. Known as the man who invented tomorrow, this French writer "took" us to the moon a hundred years before we actually landed there.

Poetry

Interested in writing poetry for young people? Take home some of the new magazines from the library, including *Hopscotch* and *New Moon*, which are looking for free verse, light verse and haiku, and *Boys' Quest*, looking for humor. They pay from $5 up to $50. The older magazines are always looking for poetry; take home some of them, too. If you have a flair for humorous poetry, try doing a book. Then run—don't walk—to get a copy of Shel Silverstein's *A Light in the Attic* or *Where the Sidewalk Ends* to see a master in the field at work.

Do Your Homework

One of the best ways to prepare yourself for writing for the juvenile market is to read some of the books recommended by eminent people in the field. At the present time, Virginia Polytechnic Institute sponsors an organization called the Children's Literature Association, which consists of teachers, librarians, authors, parents and publishers. The six hundred members are trying to encourage serious scholarship and research into the area of children's literature. In 1976, they published the names of the ten books they considered to be the best during the past two hundred years. See how many you know.

1. *Charlotte's Web* by E.B. White
2. *Where the Wild Things Are* by Maurice Sendak
3. *The Adventures of Tom Sawyer* by Mark Twain
4. *Adventures of Huckleberry Finn* by Mark Twain
5. *Little Women* by Louisa May Alcott
6. *Little House in the Big Woods* by Laura Ingalls Wilder
7. *Johnny Tremaine* by Esther Forbes
8. *The Wizard of Oz* by L. Frank Baum
9. *Little House on the Prairie* by Laura Ingalls Wilder
10. *Island of the Blue Dolphins* by Scott O'Dell

Another list of books you should be familiar with has to do with the Newberry Medal Awards given each year for an outstanding children's book. John Newberry (1713–1767), an English publisher and bookseller, was the first person to print and sell books for children. The award was created in 1921 by Frederic Melcher, chairman of the board of the R.R. Bowker Company, publishers of *Library Journal* and *Publishers Weekly*. It is presented every year by the Children's Services Division of the American Library Association. Ask your librarian for the list of winners, or check into your own set of encyclopedias at home. In the meantime, here are ten of the books that are popular with the boys and girls at my library:

1. *Lincoln: A Photobiography* by Russell Freedman (1988)
2. *Joyful Noise: Poems for Two Voices* by Paul Fleischman (1989)
3. *Number the Stars* by Lois Lowry (1990)
4. *Maniac Magee* by Jerry Spinelli (1991)
5. *Shiloh* by Phyllis Reynolds Naylor (1992)

6. *Missing May* by Cynthia Rylant (1993)
7. *The Giver* by Lois Lowry (1994)
8. *Walk Two Moons* by Sharon Creech (1995)
9. *The Midwife's Apprentice* by Karen Cushman (1996)
10. *The View From Saturday* by E.L. Konigsburg (1997)

The time may come when you can add your name to this select list of authors. Don't scoff. Many of these men and women didn't dream it could happen to them. If you have a story to tell—do it now!

 Assignment

Write down an idea for a children's book—age group eight to twelve—or a humorous poem.

8 FUN WITH FICTION FOR ADULTS

The white-haired matron in the elegant black suit stepped gingerly over the body and disappeared down the hall.

Please read this statement carefully. Find some notepaper and jot down the first thought that comes into your head. What was it? Was it the location? Did it involve the woman? The body? Can you picture the scene in your mind's eye? Good!

Now give a name to that white-haired matron. Set the scene somewhere. Describe the body lying on the hall floor. What do you think happened? Let your imagination run wild, and write about 200 words. If you have never tried to do fiction before, you may be pleasantly surprised to discover that you have a flair for writing mysteries.

During the past five or six years, I have given this premise to all of my classes to introduce them to fiction. The students usually react in the same way: They can never come up with a plot—never. A week later, many of them come into class with a big grin and admit that someone else seemed to take over their pencil or typewriter, and with a vengeance. As I have each one read his story, I sit and listen in amazement: They have become so bloodthirsty! In fact, they surprise themselves with their creative ideas concerning the matron in the elegant black suit. Here are a few excerpts from their tales of terror.

The white-haired matron in the elegant black suit stepped gingerly over the body and disappeared down the hall. I had come down the stairs just in time to see her slip her gun into her black bag and run to the nearest exit. Her victim lay in a spreading pool of blood.

(written by a senior in high school)

The white-haired matron in the elegant black suit stepped gingerly over the body and disappeared down the hall.

"Cut!" yelled the director. "We've got to do this scene again. Take your places, and make it believable this time!"

(written by a woman working on a play)

The white-haired matron in the elegant black suit stepped gingerly over the body and disappeared down the passageway toward the control room. The starship's automatic cleaning and maintenance system, sensing the inert mass in the passageway, clicked open a door from which emerged a robot.

(written by a student interested in science fiction)

The white-haired matron in the elegant black suit stepped gingerly over the body and disappeared down the dimly lit hall. No mail again today. She turned her key to open her apartment for what she knew would be the last time.

(written by an older woman living in a retirement home)

If you glance at these four responses to my premise, you can see that their backgrounds and interests color what they write. I must tell you that the "body" was also pictured by my students as a rat, a mouse and a mannequin. The students said that it was a fun assignment; some said they planned to stay in the fiction field for awhile, and to try a short story or two on their own.

Why write fiction? It could be the money you'll make if you write a blockbuster novel. Aside from that, you'll like the idea of transporting your readers to another time and another place, and creating characters that are exclusively your own. Remember, however, that fiction writing is more difficult than nonfiction, and you will have to learn some of the techniques used by professionals. But the thrill you'll derive from dreaming up plots, characters and dialogue will far outweigh the effort involved in any learning you'll have to do.

The desire to tell stories and to listen to them is inherent in human nature, and storytelling is probably the oldest of the arts. Egyptian tombs of six thousand years ago contain domestic and social tales inscribed on papyrus, and down through the corridors of time, the Greeks, Romans, Persians—all the peoples of the world—have contributed fables, legends and earthy stories. The *Tales from the Arabian Nights*, consisting of two hundred stories, came from Persia, India, Mesopotamia or Egypt; no one knows for sure. But one thing is certain: They enhanced the art of telling a story. And Bible scholars are quick to point out that this holy book is the repository of every conceivable kind of short story.

In our own country, this literary form came into being at the beginning of the nineteenth century. Edgar Allan Poe is considered the father of the American short story, and he describes it in this fashion in his "Review of Nathaniel Hawthorne's *Twice-Told Tales*":

> A skilful literary artist has constructed a tale. If wise, he has not fashioned his thought to accommodate his incidents; but having conceived, with deliberate care, a certain unique or single effect to be brought out, he then invents such incidents as may best aid him in establishing this preconceived effect.

Since that time, writers of short stories have emphasized the importance of creating a single effect, and that this kind of fiction can be compared to a portrait in miniature. It's all there, but it's compressed into an economical size. Anyone who decides to go this route must realize that she cannot do much embroidering of his characters or plot; she must constantly be on guard to shape the subject matter to get the desired effect.

Parts of a Short Story

The elements of a short story are

1. Character
2. Plot
3. Setting
4. Style, point of view, tone, mood, atmosphere and other factors in the telling of the story
5. Theme
6. Symbolism

The first three elements shouldn't give you any trouble, but let's clarify the others.

- **Style** means the selection and arrangement of words and sentences. It's the way in which a thing is said.
- **Point of view** means the relation of the storyteller to the story.
- **Tone** means the author's attitude toward his material.
- **Mood** refers to the attitude of the characters in a story toward what is happening.
- **Atmosphere** refers to the general emotional effect of a scene from a story.
- **Theme** means a brief statement of the meaning of the story— the author's message. For example, "The grass is always greener on the other side of the fence," "Revenge is sweet" or "All that glitters is not gold."
- **Symbolism** in a story emphasizes meaning on another level. In other words, are the images literal and limited to concrete experience, or do they suggest values, beliefs and ideas?

And now that that lesson is over, let's take a look at a formula for writing a short story:

character(s) → problem → complications → climax → solution

A character or characters are introduced. They meet a problem. The situation becomes more complicated and finally reaches the climactic point of tension. Then the decision is made, the problem is resolved and the story is brought to a close.

The problem faced by the character, along with its complications, is called the "rising action"; the solution, or denouement, is called the "falling action." In most stories, the "climax" line is the shortest of the three. When you write your story, keep this in mind.

Probably the best way to tell you how a short story is written is to choose a classic and analyze it using the above formula. If you've never read James Thurber's "The Catbird Seat" (first published in *The New Yorker*, November 14, 1942), you're in for a treat. The story begins:

> Mr. Martin bought the pack of Camels on Monday night in the most crowded store on Broadway. It was theater time and seven or eight men were buying cigarettes. The clerk didn't even glance at Mr. Martin, who put the pack in his overcoat pocket and went out. If any of the staff at F&S had seen him buy the cigarettes, they would have been astonished, for it was generally known that Mr. Martin did not smoke, and never had. No one saw him.

Now that the hero, or protagonist, has been introduced, we need a problem. As we read more of the story, we find out that a Mrs. Ulgine Barrows has come into the firm and is unsettling everybody with her determination to make various departments more efficient; she has, in fact, caused several people to lose their jobs. Rumor has it that she is getting ready to invade Mr. Martin's private domain and do away with some of his files. Mr. Martin decides that the only way to stop her is to rub her out. (Now we have a story going, but we need more of a *plot*.)

He goes to her apartment one night intent upon murdering her with a weapon he'll find there, but to his great dismay, he can't find any. He could use the poker or andirons, but he doesn't want to make the murder that bloody. (Now our story shows the *complication*.) What can he do? All of a sudden, a wild idea comes into his head. He sits down with brash Mrs. Barrows, accepts a highball from her and smokes a cigarette, two things he never does. Mr. Martin now schemes to get Mrs. Barrows fired by convincing the boss that she has lost her mind. He confesses to Mrs. Barrows that he smokes, drinks and takes heroin, and confides to her a fictitious plan to bump off Mr. Fitweiler, the boss. She orders him out and promises to report him to the boss the next morning. (Now we have the *crisis* of the story.) When she tells Mr. Fitweiler about Mr. Martin's smoking, drinking and threatened violence, this sounds so ridiculously out of character for the file clerk that Fitweiler thinks she needs psychiatric care and fires her. Mr. Martin returns to his beloved filing department, where he will once again be in the cat-bird seat. (This is the *climax* of the story.)

I should note that the title comes from a baseball term referring to a batter with three balls and no strikes against him, and means "sitting pretty." I should also mention to all of you amateur detectives out there that Mr. Martin bought Camel cigarettes to use as a red herring after he had rubbed out Mrs. Barrows. She smoked only Luckies; he planned to puff a few after the murder and then leave his Camel cigarette in the ashtray with hers. He never dreamed he wouldn't be able to find a weapon!

This plot can be described as one in which the hero accomplishes his goal through his own efforts. There are six or seven other basic plots often used in magazine stories, but your first attempt should revolve around the one I've discussed. If you become serious about short story writing, you may want to buy *The Writer's Digest Handbook of Short Story Writing, Vol. I & II* or *The Thirty-Six Dramatic Situations*, by George Polti, published by *The Writer*. Milton Crane, a writer who really knew the short story field, once said what makes a short story great is "the sudden unforgettable revelation of character, the vision of a world through another's eyes, the glimpse of truth and the capture of a moment in time."

If you are determined to write fiction, be aware that whether you do a story or a novel, there are three universal themes: man against man, man against nature and man against himself. The first one is used the most and is the easiest to write. The third one is psychological and requires a special kind of insight into the thoughts and desires of the protagonist.

Suppose you are all set to start your story. Will you tell it in the first person? In the third? Or will you create an omniscient observer who knows what the characters are thinking in addition to what they are doing? No matter which point of view you choose, stick with it: Your reader won't appreciate your shifting about. Hemingway did a remarkable job with a mixed point of view in "A Clean, Well-Lighted Place," but he was a master at his craft.

Now that you have chosen your own point of view (third person would be a good one to start with), let's choose a character. Let's give him some traits. How? Most writers do a composite of themselves, borrowing one or two traits from a friend or relative. Instead, why not use the signs of the zodiac? Your character could be one of the following:

- **Scorpio.** She is fascinated by religion, drugs and sex. She can be either goddess or demon.
- **Libra.** He has a compulsion to be fair and can see all sides to all questions; he is also intelligent and gullible.
- **Taurus.** She is tranquil, passive and resists change.
- **Leo.** He is proud and loves luxury, attention and ease. He rises easily to fame—unless arrogance or flattery drags him down.
- **Sagittarius.** He is innocent, filled with charisma, an idealist.

Remember: When you are creating your imaginary people, you must give them a balance; every human being is composed of good and bad characteristics. Your story will ring more truly if your hero acts like the rest of us.

How long should your story be? It can range from 1,500 to 10,000 words, with an average length of 5,000 words. You can see that in this limited form it is impossible to become philosophical in theme, or to carry out an elaborate plot. It's the economy of the short story that makes it such a challenge to a writer—to stay within bounds and yet produce a great piece of fiction.

Have you ever thought of writing a short-short? These run about 1,500 words and are ideal for those who can't spend too much time at the typewriter. But don't picture it as a sketch or a vignette. Short-shorts contain all of the elements of the regular short story: the opening, the introduction of the problem, the intensification of the conflict, the crisis and the resolution. But you will have to cut down on your descriptions and dialogue, and use succinct phrases instead of paragraphs to get necessary information across.

This kind of writing isn't a breeze, so start now to read some magazines that feature a short-short from time to time. You'll soon get the feel of it and see how quickly the author gets into the story and how he makes you believe that it conveys the same impact as a full-length short story. If you are successful at this type of fiction, you can expect a check for $750 or more from some of the slick magazines.

As you get ready to write your story of adventure, love, mystery, horror or science fiction, here are several other helpful hints.

1. When you begin your story, introduce your character, setting and problem in the first few paragraphs. Your reader wants to know what is going on as soon as possible. Most writers today conform to this rule; get into the habit of doing so with your stories.

2. Your dialogue should move the plot forward, which means your characters should make statements that fill us in a bit more on the story line or the people in the story.

3. Try to find a title for your story that fits. What famous novel started out with these working titles?
   Tomorrow Is Another Day
   Baa! Baa! Black Sheep
   Tote the Weary Load
   Not in Our Stars
   Milestones
   Bugles Sang True
   Jettison
   Have you come up with an answer? You may not believe it, but these were the tentative titles of *Gone With the Wind*.

4. Make sure you do an outline or a framework for your story.

5. Make sure you have a theme.

6. Make sure the story contains a conflict.

7. The reader should care about your lead character.

8. Your story should give the reader an emotional experience.

9. Your story should not contain too many coincidences.

10. Has something changed in your story? If your character or characters are still the same, you don't have a story.

Suppose you have read all of this material, and yet you dream of writing a novel. Should you do it? A better question is: Can you do it? From what I have gathered, it is easier to write a novel than a short story, but don't believe it is a matter of adding more characters and a greatly expanded plot. Writing a novel can be compared to creating scenes in a movie: Each one gives dramatic information through the characters. That means, of course, that you will know your characters inside out; you'll know what they think and do, and why they act the way they do.

Now comes the question of what you should write about.

Story ideas come from the world around us. Theodore Dreiser found the story of *An American Tragedy* in the newspaper (trial and all). Nathaniel Hawthorne was rummaging through the attic of an old custom house one day and came across a package of *A*s cut out of red cloth. He knew the letter *A* was sewn to the dress of an adulteress in those days. He stood there visualizing how a young girl would feel—and then wrote his masterpiece. Daniel Defoe, the author of *Robinson Crusoe*, heard of someone stranded on a desert island. He asked himself what he would do. How could he survive?

What kind of novel should you write? Here is a short list.

Autobiographical	Romance
Adventure	Satire
Mystery/detective	Technothriller
Fantasy	Technothriller
Social	Horror & supernatural
Humor	Gothic

No matter what kind of novel you write, the parts are:
- Characters
- Setting
- Plot
- Point of view

If you write a novel, the editor will expect you to send the first three chapters and a synopsis. Here is a sample of a synopsis I've done for a teenage novel I hope to sell some day. (This is the first page; it runs to ten pages, but editors usually want only seven to eight pages.)

Synopsis of "The Ghost of Whispering Pines."

When sixteen-year old Laurie O'Neill is invited to spend part of the summer at her aunt's inn in southern Virginia, she is delighted. She is very close to Aunt Kate, and this will give her a chance to be with her and to make some money as a waitress. It will also give her the opportunity to put her ESP to work. She has more than her share of extrasensory perception ever since an injury to her head years ago.

Aunt Kate has told her that she needs her expertise in finding out why Amanda, the beautiful ghost from the Civil War, is no longer content to appear in her filmy white wedding dress throughout the inn or along the roads nearby or in Evergreen Cemetery. Why? . . .

Note that this synopsis is in the present tense. After you write your first one, it will be easier. If you write it before your manuscript is finished, it will act as a guide to your story line.

A bit of advice: Take a course or two on writing a novel, and read some books on the subject. You can't do it without some help along the way.

 Assignment

Now is the time to write a page or two of the romance or mystery you've always wanted to do. Go with the flow—don't try to tear it apart early in the game.

9 OF COURSE YOU CAN WRITE A COLUMN!

Years ago when Heloise Cruse, an Air Force wife, moved to Hawaii, she found time on her hands and decided to look for a part-time job. She toyed with the idea of writing a column devoted to household hints she had picked up from her own experiences for the *Honolulu Advertiser*. The editor told her politely that he wasn't interested. Undaunted, Heloise asked him several more times, and he finally agreed to hire her and pay her $10 a week for "Hints From Heloise." The rest is history: In three years' time, the *Honolulu Advertiser*'s circulation went from 46,000 to 71,000. A few years later, Heloise's column appeared in syndication in over five hundred newspapers. She went on to write several books, and received many awards for her clever domestic ideas. According to reliable sources, she eventually earned $100,000 a year—and to think it all started with a weekly column! When she died in 1977, her daughter took over, and "Hints From Heloise" is still going strong.

Abigail Van Buren and her sister, Ann Landers, started their columns because they were concerned about the many problems faced by young and old alike. They never dreamed that their advice would take off like a skyrocket and make them known on a national and international level. At first their columns were simple, with suggestions on how to cope with routine, everyday problems, but in later years they discussed a variety of sensitive subjects with guidelines from clergymen, doctors, lawyers, counselors, psychiatrists and even economists. In fact, Ann Landers wrote a book in 1978 called *The Ann Landers Encyclopedia*. It covered subjects ranging from abortion to zoonosis, a disease man can acquire from animals. When she started doing her column for the *Chicago Sun-Times* in 1955, she didn't realize how popular it would be and that many readers would take her sage advice—and chuckle over the foibles of humanity. Both sisters write with a sense of humor which seems to temper the grim realities presented in many of the letters.

The name Erma Bombeck evokes a lightheartedness that brightens every nook and cranny. I'm sure her column, "At Wit's End," was created as a defense against the drudgery of everyday tasks and raising a family in suburbia. It began in 1964, and one year later it went into syndication. Several years later, she decided to put her columns into a book. It did so well that she did five more, including the number-one best-seller, *If Life Is a Bowl of Cherries, What Am I Doing in the Pits?* She died in 1996, and at that time, her column was in seven hundred newspapers and she had written fourteen books.

Art Buchwald started out working for an American newspaper while living in Paris. He, too, didn't have an inkling that he would eventually win world recognition for his column and from his books, all written with the kind of wit that tickles our funny-bone. I'll never forget one of his columns, written in 1974, that told about his taking to heart President Ford's pronouncement that we all had to bite the bullet on the economy. He decided to go down to his local sporting goods store and buy a bullet as soon as possible. But when he told the clerk what he wanted, the man said, "You mean a box of bullets." Art Buchwald told him that one would be enough. This conversation followed:

"What kind of bullet do you want?"
"I don't know. Are there different kinds?"
"Of course. What kind of gun do you have?" he asked.

"I don't have a gun," I said.

"Then what do you want a bullet for?"

"I want to bite on it," I admitted sheepishly.

(Los Angeles Times Syndicate, 1974)

The rest of the column was just as hilarious as the beginning—only a master of his craft could make a serious subject so amusing. Humor, by the way, is the most difficult kind of writing to do, and very few men and women have succeeded in this field.

Are you interested in food and cooking? You don't have to be Julia Child or Craig Claiborne to establish yourself as a columnist in this category. A friend of mine, Jane Mengenhauser, can vouch for that. Jane had worked on the staff of several newspapers, and had written features on food for the *Washington Post* as a free-lancer, but hoped some day to do a column on recipes and cooking. Several years ago, she heard that the *Alexandria* (VA) *Journal* was looking for reporters. She took six sample columns on food into the editor's office and convinced him to hire her as columnist. He did so, and a short time later, circulation of his five *Journal* newspapers mushroomed.

Can a novice ever become a columnist? It's elementary, my dear Watson. There isn't one of you out there reading this book who doesn't have some expertise on some subject. Your best bet is to query an editor of a weekly newspaper, and send him five or six columns running about 350 words each. Also, add a rundown of some other aspects of your subject that you plan to do later on. (You must convince the editor that you won't bog down after writing up some of your thoughts and ideas.) Don't expect to do all of your columns off the top of your head: Go to the library for more information and angles. Choose a catchy title if you can. And this is the time to scour the writer's magazines for new publications in the need of ideas for columns. Your life as a columnist could begin tomorrow—well, almost.

My first column materialized when I'd returned to the States and was living in Arlington, Virginia. After two years in Japan and three in Germany, I felt service wives overseas needed to know what was going on back home. I queried John Wiant, an editor with *American Weekend*, and he thought I had a good idea. It was then that "Back Home" came into being. One of my first columns reported that people back home were busy visiting art galleries, rereading the classics, setting the dinner table the European way, dancing the Bossa Nova, taking art lessons and writing their memoirs.

This weekly column traveled all over the world. I did it for eighteen months, and it gave me my most important lesson in writing: self discipline. Neither rain nor sleet nor a toothache nor a sore toe could interfere with meeting a deadline. One of the nicest compliments I ever received was from an army officer I bumped into one day after he had returned from Korea. He told me that the minute he got a copy of the paper, he turned to my column to see what was going on back home.

Several years later, I had a chance to do another column called "A Woman's World" for the *Arlington News*. I wrote it every week for thirteen years and covered food, fashions, TV, movies, books, cooking, biography, travel, household hints and famous women.

Of course it was the best thing that ever could have happened to me. Those early years of column writing had only made me a great researcher; the later years transformed me into a writer. I somehow managed to write about such things as recipes from Peg Bracken's *I Hate To Cook Book*, which included her famous Stayabed Stew, a tasty concoction thrown together and into a slow oven while the cook catches up on her reading; how to pretend you've been to the Cordon Bleu cooking school in Paris by adding tarragon to your scrambled eggs, a bit of brandy to your pumpkin pie or some savory to your meatloaf; how to cut your food bill by shopping after a meal, leaving your husband at home, making a list, using coupons and checking the ads; and paying heed to Julia Child's suggestion to use your senses when you go to the store and snap the beans, pop the peapods, rub the cabbage leaves and so on.

Before you get the impression that my column was centered only around food, I also did material on the history of fashion; the new trends in education; how to lose pounds and keep them off; how to become a successful speaker; how to write effective publicity for your club; how to get unusual program ideas if you've been elected

85

chairman; the pros and cons of watching TV; how to fight depression during the holiday season; the thrill of visiting Lion Country Safari near Richmond, Virginia, and peering at the wild animals through your (closed) car windows; what it was like to wine and dine during Roman times; the curse of the legendary Hope diamond; and how to choose the right kind of clothing to complement your figure.

From time to time, I featured a column on household hints. Why? Because my readers told me they enjoyed reading them, and many of them said they cut them out and taped them to the refrigerator door. Here are five I especially like.

- Straight pins will go through material more easily if you use a cake of soap as a pincushion.
- Water rings in fabric will disappear if rubbed gently with a silver spoon or coin.
- Milk of magnesia will take the itch out of poison ivy-infected skin.
- To prevent dripping fat from flaring up and ruining a steak or chicken when barbecuing, place lettuce leaves over the hot coals.
- Nail polish remover can be used to clean the type on a typewriter. It will not harm the metal and dries instantly.

If you reread the last few pages covering my column ideas, you'll realize that I have mentioned topics that could be written by many would-be columnists. Once you become established with a newspaper and an editor, you'll be allowed more leeway in what you can write about, and you may even find that you will be allowed to do an occasional straight piece of journalism. Begin to beat the bushes now for a weekly newspaper that may be interested in what you have to offer.

Topics to Consider

Just in case you haven't found a subject that is your cup of tea, here is a list of fifty topics that might be more to your liking.

Advice	Humor
Antiques	Idea Exchange

Armchair Travels	It's a Fact!
Astrology	Knit One, Purl Two
Bridge	Know Your Wines
Car Care	Miniatures
Child Care	Movies
Club Notes	News for Women
Coin Collecting	Nostalgia
Collectibles	Nutrition
Commentary	Over 40
Cooking Tips	Pet Care
Down on the Farm	Plant Care
Education	Politics
Elderhostel Programs	Radio
Financial Advice	Retirement Hints
Footnotes to History	Sewing
Freebies	Shopper's Guide
GardeningGolden Age	Social Activities
Gourmet the Easy Way	Sports
Handicrafts	Stamp Collecting
Health	Theater
Hooked on Books	Travel Tips
Household Repairs	TV

Getting Started

As soon as an idea for a column begins to perk in your mind, write down the various aspects of it immediately: Don't let those thoughts slip away. Let's suppose you are going to write about cooking, a subject in which you have some expertise. Aside from sharing a number of delicious and unusual recipes with your readers, what else can you offer? Since most editors expect you to send them five or six sample columns, you'll have to produce a variety of things to talk about.

This is the time to use your ingenuity. One of your sample columns could tell the story of Apicius, the Roman gourmet who wrote the first cookbook almost two thousand years ago. Another could discuss the free cookbooks available from certain processed-food distributors. Still another could feature a typical dinner served at Mount Vernon by the Washingtons. Two or three could highlight cooking shortcuts and facts on proper nutrition. You could also give advice on microwave cooking.

With these samples in hand, you should be able to convince the editor of a weekly newspaper that you can communicate with a readership for a long time. Many people like to read about food, even if they make every effort to stay out of the kitchen. Mention that fact to the editor, and you may find yourself hired.

Then what? After your column takes off, make plans to extend its publication. If your weekly circulates in a limited area, you can reach out to other newspapers in the state. Send them half a dozen tearsheets (samples of your column taken directly from the paper) with a cover letter. You can find a list of newspapers in the *Editor & Publisher Yearbook* or *Working of the Nation* at your main library; they will also give you the circulation, editor's name and other vital facts. Make sure to send a SASE with your query.

Later, when you think it's time to try a syndicate, go through the same process. Once again, tell the editor what you have in mind and why his readers would be interested in your material. But this time you'll have an edge: Your published columns will add credibility to your qualifications.

After doing a column for fifteen years for local publications, I can assure you it is one of the most rewarding types of writing. You'll be asked to speak at luncheons, you'll receive fan mail and you'll be invited to many social gatherings. And best of all, you'll see your writing become more professional and act as a stepping stone to other creative ideas.

 Assignment

Choose a subject for a weekly column—maybe "Hooked on Books." Write five or six pieces covering trends, stories about writers—now and from the past, or what books to look for at a book sale. Each column should be about 500 words.

10 IT COULD FILL A BOOK

An idea for a book was practically handed to me one Sunday afternoon in the summer of 1961 when I attended a reception at Fort Benning, Georgia, for new officers and their wives. Many of the young women I met confessed they were a bit bewildered by the strange new world they had entered, and wished they had a guidebook that could explain army life in a simple fashion. (They were reading one, but it overwhelmed them with too many details.)

When I met a good friend of mine later in the week, I asked her if she would like to do a lighthearted guidebook with me. She agreed at once, and we were off and running. She was the "Auntie Mame" type, witty and funny and always full of amusing anecdotes to tell. We sat on my front porch one morning and exchanged ideas for the book and dreams about fame and fortune waiting for us around the bend. Oh, sure!

We soon discovered that it was one thing to do skits at luncheons, but quite another to put those words to paper. We finally came up with a title, *This Is the Army, Mrs. Jones*, and planned to do a preface together and then do ten chapters. What chapters? We had subject titles, but that was it. We didn't dare say that we didn't have the slightest idea of how to put a book together.

Somehow we managed to chug along and finished five chapters. Now what?

At this point, we thought it was time to approach a publisher or two, but found that our friends and relatives had no ready contacts. Finally, we went over to see someone on post who worked in public relations and who gave us the names of two places in New York City. I sent off two letters explaining our little project, but in both instances the answer was a flat no. Thelma and I refused to quit, and the day came when a company in Charlotte, North Carolina, took us on. We couldn't believe it—somebody was willing to gamble that we could write a successful book!

And then it happened. Thelma's husband received orders to go to Paris within a few short weeks. We vowed that we would do the book by mail: Nothing could stop us now. Thelma sent me material so that I could put it all together and make the publisher happy with the results. After almost two years of work, the galleys came in the mail, and I knew that *This Is the Army, Mrs. Jones* was on its way to being published.

If you're wondering what galleys are, it's your typeset book on long narrow sheets of paper, waiting for you to check any errors. I received three sets and was told to give the other two to friends capable of proofreading. Later, I was to compare their findings with mine. I couldn't dawdle: All copies had to be mailed back in ten days.

The book was published in paperback and distributed to post exchanges in the United States and overseas. I'll never forget the thrill of seeing my first copy. Eventually, the *Army Times* gave it a favorable review, and CBS News came down to do a radio interview for its "Weekend" show. But the greatest thrill for me was when my cadet son walked into the bookstore at West Point and spied *This Is the Army, Mrs. Jones*.

If you have never been introduced to army life, you may be wondering what the handbook was all about. Thelma and I described what it was like to live on an army post; how to cope with army abbreviations; what to take to Alaska, Hawaii or Germany; the sequence in rank; how to seat people at a formal dinner party; how to create a gourmet meal in no time; and how to be a successful program chairman. We provided all kinds of recipes and forty different entertainment ideas the new army wives could use when it was their turn to do a program at the club.

But where we helped the most was in the section that interpreted what their husbands would say to them from time to time. Here is an excerpt.

> Suppose your husband comes home for lunch one day and says, "Honey, we had a C & S meeting this morning at the Battle Group CP, and the old man announced that my company is going on a three-day FTX." You can see it's almost like a new language.

Thelma and I decided it was important to list at least sixty of these terms and abbreviations. We also added the Army's unique way of telling time so that Mrs. Jones would know that 2400 (twenty-four hundred hours) means midnight and that 0600 (oh-six hundred hours) means 6 A.M.

Using Your Own Experiences

I've gone into some detail about this handbook to show all of you that there may be something in your own experience that can be shared with a number of readers. This informal paperback never became a bestseller, but it stayed in print for seven or eight years, and a copy turned up last year at a flea market nearby. During the past few years, the Army has become less demanding in its protocol and club functions, and I hear that many of the wives now hold down jobs in town, or even on post. In my day, this kind of freedom was almost unheard of. But I am sure that parts of *This Is the Army, Mrs. Jones* could still help service wives planning to follow their military men all over the world.

My handbook was a nonfiction book. Do you have material in your background that could lend itself to a book of this kind? I found a number of men and women in my classes, and others I read about, that write nonfiction and managed to find a publisher. Here are their ideas.

Are you in one of the services? Keep a journal or diary and see if you can write an interesting account of your life here or in a foreign country. But realize that being in the service itself won't sell the book. Your story must fill a need or be so extra special that many people will buy a copy and tell others about it. Years ago, an army wife in Japan wrote a book called *Over the Bamboo Fence* that sold quite well, but she wrote it when the customs of that country weren't too well known. In 1979, a young graduate of West Point, Lucian Truscott, wrote his first mystery, *Dress Gray*, using his alma mater as the setting. A retired general who lives near here keeps himself busy by writing paperbacks on battles of the Civil War; this area is steeped in history of that period in America's past.

Are you a teacher? Can you write about your experiences in working with your students? Bel Kaufman did that in 1964 when she wrote *Up the Down Staircase*. She used her background as a teacher in a New York City school and fictionalized her story. She added her special touch by building her story line from administrative memos, student compositions and interschool communications. Later it was made into a first-rate movie.

Another teacher, Jenny Gray, wrote a guidebook for new teachers and called it *The Teacher's Survival Guide, or How to Teach Teen-agers and Live to Tell About It*. She wrote it while living in California, and had it published by Fearon Publishers of Palo Alto. You may want to look around for a nearby publisher when you do your first book. (You can find some listed in *Writer's Market*.) I don't know Ms. Gray personally, but I do know she went on to write *Teaching Without Tears* a year or two later. She had to be doing something right.

Have you ever heard of William C. Anderson? He's a retired Air Force officer who wrote *Home Sweet Home on Wheels*, which tells about the adventures he and his wife experienced traveling in an RV for almost a year. He is also the author of *Hurricane Hunters*, *The Great Bicycle Expedition* and *When the Offspring Have Sprung*. I should mention that his RV book not only relates his travels but also gives advice on motor home and RV living. Have you taken trips during the past few years that would make interest-

92

ing reading? Think about it. If you're planning a trip around the world, start your journal now. By the time you return, you'll have enough material on hand to fill a book.

Are you a walker? Aaron Sussman and Ruth Goode wrote a book about ten years ago and called it *The Magic of Walking*. They added that extra something by including excerpts on walking by famous men and women in literature. They quote "The Open Road" by Walt Whitman, "The Pleasure of Walking" by Oliver Wendell Holmes, "Departure" by Edna St. Vincent Millay, "The Pedestrian" by Ray Bradbury and "The Road Not Taken" by Robert Frost. Find this book at the library. If you have never been thrilled at the thought of going for a walk, you will be when you read this book. If you are already a walker, you may get an idea for a book of your own.

Can your family provide you with material for a book? Begin now to write down some of the things that happened in your childhood. Sam Levenson did, and in his successful book *Everything But Money*, he told about his upbringing in a family of eight brothers and sisters in such a way that he became a popular writer and TV personality. His tales of Jewish life on the Lower East Side of New York will be remembered for a long time. Jean Kerr won recognition when she wrote about her children in *Please Don't Eat the Daisies* and *The Snake Has All the Lines*. If you bemoan the fact that you can't get any writing done around the house because it's so noisy, follow Kerr's example: She usually drove her car down a block or two, parked and dug out her writing gear. Shirley Jackson, famous for her gothic tales, wrote about her growing family in *My Life Among the Savages*; it's worth reading for its hilarious moments, but also to show you a side to this author's writing that isn't too well known.

Have you ever thought of doing a cookbook? Peg Bracken did, and produced *The I Hate To Cook Book*, filled with 180 quick and easy (and unusual) recipes, along with advice about kitchen problems. She slanted her book toward the housewife who felt hostile toward the kitchen. She was amazed at how many women bought her book. They liked her humor—and her tasty dishes. Norma Jean and Carol Darden wrote a delightful cookbook, now in paperback, called *Spoon Bread and Strawberry Wine*, which contains the recipes and reminiscences of the sisters' family, stretching back to the days before the Civil War.

Several years ago, some senior citizens in Wisconsin, who entered the "Yarns of Yesteryear" contest sponsored by the University of Wisconsin Extension Division and the Regional Writers Association, had a great idea. They took nearly a hundred of their glimpses of the past and put them into a book called *We Were Children Then*. It did so well that other compilations are in the offing.

Verna Mae Slone wrote a simple, moving account of her life in the hills and hollows of Kentucky for her grandchildren and called it *What My Heart Wants to Tell*. Her purpose was to dispel the unflattering myth of the "hillbilly," and she traced the hard life of her family as they forced subsistence out of a stubborn and hostile land. Another grandmother, Juretta Murray, wrote a book that told about the wonderful world of astronomy for her grandchildren. She called it *Listen, Look, the Stars!* and wrote it in the form of talks to her granddaughters. Her aim in writing the book was to tie the stars to thoughts of God, and to show that friendship with the stars is a fascinating experience. She was able to use her hobby in a different way.

One of the most unusual books I have found while working on this chapter is *The Storybook Cookbook*. Carol MacGregor had the ingenious idea of selecting twenty-two delicious concoctions mentioned in the classics of children's literature and providing recipes for them. For example, *Misty of Chincoteague*, by Marguerite Henry features Chincoteague Pot Pie; *Hans Brinker or The Silver Skates* gives a recipe for waffles; and *Treasure Island* describes how to make chipped beef. The author prefaced each recipe with the paragraph or two that contained the reference to the food, and provided her young readers with step-by-step instructions on preparing it.

The year 1977 will always be an important one to Paula Delfield of Brownsville, Wisconsin: She celebrated her golden wedding anniversary and the birth of her first great-grandchild, and saw her first book come into being. It took her three years of research and writing to finish *The Indian Priest*, a true story of a young man in her town, and she had it accepted after the third try. She is now doing another book, and plans to keep writing books and articles far into the future.

One of the funniest ideas for a book happened to Arue Szura in Castro Valley, California. She burned so many meals that her family—and local firemen—named her "The Carbon Queen." When she enrolled in an adult writing class, she decided to make the most of the good-natured kidding going on around her by writing a cookbook. She called it *Where There's Smoke There's Dinner*, and included a number of recipes from the firemen. After being turned down by several publishers, she came to the conclusion that her book didn't appeal to them because it had too much of a local slant. She then took it to a print shop and ordered five hundred copies made. She distributed them to local bookstores and gift shops, and sent out mail orders through one of the newspapers. In ten weeks the books were gone. When a revised edition was printed, Arue Szura set up a booth at a carnival in San Francisco where she sold and autographed copies of the new version. She can still remember how embarrassing it was to have fire engines come roaring down her street to put out her kitchen fires, but is pleased that something negative can be turned into something positive.

Query First

Suppose the day comes when you have chosen your idea for a nonfiction book. How should you go about collecting your material? What does an editor look for? How can you convince her that your book will sell? Should you send a query letter or a more detailed book proposal?

Many editors prefer to see a one-page query first. If you choose to go this route, make sure to give the theme or focus of your book in the first paragraph. Follow this with some details on the potential market for your material, and why you believe you are qualified to write this book. You can end your letter with some of your credits, if you have any.

If you receive a favorable response, you can send off a detailed proposal and a more definitive market analysis. You should also include two or three completed chapters and an outline of the rest of your book; actually, the outline is a number of chapter synopses. You will have to name your chapters and do a summary of each one. If you're thinking that all of this adds up to quite a bit of work, you're right. But the editor must be convinced that she is accepting a book that will have sales potential and that she will not lose a great deal of money.

Remember one thing when you query about your book: Use a narrative hook, if possible, so the editor will want to keep reading. Your idea will be in competition with many others, and you will have to offer something fresh and different to catch her attention.

If all of this information is just what you've been looking for, you may still need some help that's crucial to your book idea. What publishers will be interested in the kind of material you're rounding up? To make sure that the book you have in mind is of the same type published by the house to which you are sending it, take a trip to the library and find *Literary Marketplace*, compiled by Bowker, and thumb through its pages. Here you'll find the addresses of publishers, names of editors, a brief description of the type of books published and the number of books they do per year. You should also do some browsing in the bookstores to see what is on the market.

Even though you are a beginning writer, it isn't too soon to start a diary or journal to which you can refer later on. I can vouch for the fact that the day will come when you will have enough bits of information to get started on a book. If it happened to me, it can happen to you.

 Assignment

Here is the moment for you to start that book you've been thinking about. A love story? A children's picture book? A cookbook? Write some key words.

11 ARE YOU ON TARGET WITH YOUR MARKET?

I'll always remember a man named Sam. In his seventies, he was a member of a writing group in Falls Church, Virginia, who usually had a little success story to tell every week. Every week! But I could soon see why he received little checks and encouraging words from fiction and nonfiction editors.

He walked around with a copy of the current *Writer's Market* always tucked under his arm. Whenever he wrote an article or a short story, he went through this book with an eagle eye, searching for the magazine that seemed suitable for his piece. On top of that, he kept a ledger that had all of the details about the article or short story, who bought it or rejected it and other markets that he would also try—if it was rejected. Even though more and more writers are now looking at the market first and gearing their manuscripts to fit into it, Sam did very well with his method—maybe old-fashioned, but it suited him. One point he always emphasized: He always sent a SASE.

Market Analysis

As you begin to produce material, you'll find that you have a tendency to latch onto the markets that happen to be on hand. A new one appears in the latest writer's magazine, or one of your friends tells you he's made a sale and why don't you try them too. But if you're hoping to find a home for your article on raising white orchids, it won't be with your friend's publication that deals with home improvements. If you're sending out fiction, make sure you aren't aiming at a nonfiction market. According to many editors, this happens fairly often.

What's the best way to become familiar with publications? As I've mentioned before, you will be amazed at the number of new magazines and newspapers available. Most of them can be bought at drugstores and supermarkets. Buy some of the ones that appeal to you and read them thoroughly to get the feel of the style used in each one.

If you want to build a library of magazines at home, go to yard sales and flea markets. Watch for your public library to have a book and magazine sale, where you can pick up a variety of published material for a nominal sum. Exchange magazines with your friends, especially those who belong to writer's clubs. We have been doing this lately in several of my groups, and it has helped tremendously in getting us acquainted with current needs in fiction and nonfiction—and of course we're saving all kinds of money.

But even if you follow through with these suggestions, you must do a bit more. Send for some of the sample magazines and newspapers mentioned in *Writer's Digest* and *The Writer*. Some of them will be free; others will cost a dollar or two. When you send for them, ask for the free writer's guidelines that are usually available.

Coping With Rejection

One of the most important tips I have given in this book should be repeated here: Don't send out one manuscript and then sit back and wait for results. Once you send out an article or a story, it will, of course, take time to do another one. But let an idea take shape as soon as possible, and let it grow in your mind a little every day. In fiction, especially, get under the skin of your characters so that you know them almost as well as you know yourself. In the meantime, protect yourself from a possible rejection of your submission by training yourself to send out a filler or two every week. Later on, you can send out several articles or stories instead, if you wish. But for now, get into the habit of dropping a recipe or a footnote to history into the mail at least once a week.

Once you start writing, you'll find out that rejection slips come in all shapes, sizes and colors. Some of the messages are terse and read:

> Thank you very much for your recent submission. Unfortunately, it does not suit our current editorial needs.

or

> Thank you for inquiring as to our interest in your project. Unfortunately, it does not sound particularly well-suited to our list.

But many of them sound like this:

> Thank you for sending your manuscript to be considered for publication. It has not, however, been selected for publication and is being returned.
>
> We would be happy for the chance to look over your other work which you feel would be suitable for our magazine.

Then there are some that have a personal note written by the editor telling the writer to keep them in mind for other articles or story possibilities. Keep these in a special place on your desk. Something in your manuscript caught the fancy of the individual in charge.

One of the nicest rejection slips I have ever received read:

> Thank you for allowing Children's Press to hold your manuscript, *The Pumpkin People*. The editors were impressed with your work.

We regret that we must return this material. This in no way reflects upon your work. Your writing is excellent, and it is obvious that you have thoroughly researched your subject. After extensive editorial discussion, it was decided to return your material because it is not suited to our present publishing program. Children's Press rarely publishes an individual book. . . .

Thank you again for allowing us to review your work.

One of the most humorous turndowns came from an in-flight magazine, *TWA Ambassador*. I plan to try them again because those editors have a funny-bone. They sent a two-part card which read:

Rejection Slip (Re-jek-shun-slip) n., A verbal crutch used by editors who are too busy and/or lazy to write a personal letter or comment when they refuse to buy a perfectly good manuscript that a smarter editor would snap up in a minute.

That's what a rejection slip is, and that's what this card is. We'd rather write a letter and tell you why we aren't going to buy your work. But if we did that with all the manuscripts we receive, we wouldn't have time left to request checks for the few we do buy.

And you wouldn't like that.

So don't take this rejection slip personally, and feel free to query again or send more manuscripts. We look at them all. And when we find one that fits exactly what we want, we send another form reply.

A check.

You'll like that even better than a nice letter.

The Editors

Whenever I read this card to my students, they always laugh at its lighthearted approach to one phase of writing that is often unpleasant. But they appreciate my following up with some of the reasons why editors won't accept the material in front of them.

You've already been told some of them, but let's look at a few more:

1. You have exceeded the word limit. It doesn't matter if you tack on 40 or 50 words to a 1,000-word article or story, but if you add 110 to 120 words, you could be in trouble. If you're more than 10 percent over the limit, this could be a reason for your submission's returning home. Keep in mind that editors have word limits because their space is restricted, and they can only use so many pieces.

2. Your material is too trite. If you're doing a story about a typical family complete with a dog and a cat, add those special touches that make them all a little different from the ones we read about every day. Give them a problem and a solution that hasn't been done again and again.

3. Your material is too wordy. There are too many adjectives and adverbs; you've used words that need explanation or should be said more simply.

4. Your story lacks a good plot or theme.

5. Your story sounds contrived in its development.

6. The lead of your article does not grab the reader's attention.

7. Your article needs more facts and research.

8. The magazine has assigned a similar piece to another writer.

9. The magazine has a similar story on hand.

10. The editors believe this subject has been overdone.

The story is told (all true) that in the winter of 1843–1844 in New York City, a dark, slender man with a look of shabby elegance visited the offices of *Graham's Magazine*, where he had once worked for several months. He submitted some verses he had written to his former boss. The man looked them over and shook his head. Then he asked some of the staff in his office to take a look. They agreed with him, but took up a collection of $15.00 to help their former colleague, who told them that he and his young wife were nearly destitute. The poem? "The Raven," written by Edgar Allan Poe.

Many other famous men and women had to cope with rejection slips, including Thomas Wolfe, Norman Mailer, Joyce Carol Oates and John Updike: even Emily Dickinson's poetry was ridiculed by Houghton Mifflin after her death. As I mentioned before, you can cope by sending out several of your creations so that you are not waiting for the mailman every day, hoping you've made a sale and finally have a byline.

When rejected material does come back, look it over critically, and, if you think it still sounds pretty good, mail it out again immediately. In fact, send it to six or seven publications. If it becomes dog-eared in the meantime, retype it. If the day comes when you know you can improve it, analyze what is wrong and revise it.

A Chinese Editor Rejects a Manuscript

Illustrious brother of the sun and moon: Behold thy servant prostrate before thy feet. I kowtow to thee and beg of thy graciousness thou mayest grant that I may speak and live. Thy honored manuscript has deigned to cast the light of its august countenance upon me. With raptures I have perused it. By the bones of my ancestors, never have I encountered such wit, such pathos, such lofty thoughts. With fear and trembling, I return the writing. Were I to publish the treasure you sent me, the Emperor would order that it should be made the standard, and that none be published except such as equaled it. Knowing literature as I do, and that it would be impossible in ten thousand years to equal what you have done, I send your writing back. Ten thousand times I crave your pardon. Behold, my head is at your feet. Do what you will.

Your servant's servant
The Editor

Even though you couldn't help but smile at this unique and extra-polite rejection, you are going to be unhappy when your creation comes back—maybe again and again. But take heart. It has happened to many other writers—even famous ones, who forged ahead and began to sell their manuscripts.

Now is the time to join a writer's club in your area, where you can meet other writers and learn about markets and publications. Eventually, attend a writer's conference that will feature speakers who interest you. The May issues of *Writer's Digest* and *The Writer* showcase upcoming writers conferences and other events every year. It is worth your while to go to one of them. You will meet editors and publishers, and network with other writers, both experienced and wannabes.

Check out *Byline Magazine* in the *Writer's Market*. Its editors are especially interested in writers getting their first byline. And remember, every issue of *Writer's Digest* and *The Writer* can be found in almost every library and in many bookstores throughout the country.

 Assignment

You have just received your first rejection slip. Will you rewrite your piece—or try a new article or story?

12 SENDING YOUR MANUSCRIPT

One of the greatest moments in your life as a new writer will take place on the day you send your creative offspring into the big wide world of publishing. But before you do that, give it a fighting chance to make a good impression, no matter where it goes. You can help immensely by making sure you have done all you can before it sets off on its journey.

Many of you, no doubt, have made the switch from a typewriter to a word processor or a computer. After several days of bewilderment, you have discovered how much easier your life has become. You can now have your words counted, be offered synonyms from a thesaurus or be given a choice of typeface to print out your material. But best of all, if you need to make changes, you can do so without typing the whole page over again.

No matter what you are writing on, your goal should be to produce pages of clean, error-free copy. When you are ready for your final draft, make sure your paper is 20-pound bond. This paper has a touch of quality about it, and seems to hold up better than the other kinds.

If you use a computer in your work, make sure that the right side of your manuscript has a ragged print edge. Editors do not want that side to be justified.

The Final Draft

Let's suppose the time has come for you to do your final draft. Pay close attention to the first page of your manuscript: It will separate you from the know-nothings. First of all, don't use any kind of cover sheet. Editors want to see that top page immediately. In the upper left corner, type your name and address, including ZIP code, on three single-spaced lines. Then move over to the extreme right and type the approximate number of words, using an abbreviation so that it reads "Appr. 850 words." If you are worried about the rights you are selling, it may be wise not to specify rights on your first page. Some editors may think it a bit presumptuous on your part as a beginning writer to make that statement. It might be wise to wait until you have picked up some credits.

Next, about one-third of the way down the page, type the title in capital letters (make sure it is centered) with the word "by" beneath it (also centered) and your name or pen name under that. Each item should be double-spaced. Never number the first page.

Moving right along, after typing your title and byline, drop down three double spaces, indent five letter spaces, and begin your article or story. All of your paragraphs should be indented five spaces throughout your material. Margins should be 1¼ inches on all sides of each page, except, of course, for page 1. And remember, all of your work must be double-spaced.

Pages should be numbered in the upper right-hand corner. Your surname or a key word from your title should appear in the upper left; if a page or two should stray from the manuscript, it will be a simple matter to identify it. When you get to the end of your manuscript, drop down about three double spaces and type "The End." Center it so that it presents a neat appearance.

If you decide not to specify your rights on the first page of your manuscript, you should become familiar with some of the terms used in this business of writing and selling. Here are a few definitions.

- **First North American serial rights** means that a magazine is buying the exclusive right to publish the material for the first time and only once.
- **Second serial rights** gives the magazine the right to reprint the

material once after its original publication.
- **All periodical rights** means that the magazine is buying the exclusive right to print and reprint the material here and in foreign countries.

Someday, when you have sold a book, you will have to sign a contract, which will tell you in detail the rights the publisher is buying and the ones that belong to you.

As you whip your manuscript into shape, take a breather and send off a query letter to two or three publishers. Reread chapter six, on article writing, to see once again how it is done. But when you write a query letter, make sure it is typed and single-spaced, and don't forget that SASE. You have already learned how important a query letter can be; look through your manuscript, and start your letter with the most intriguing item it contains. Make that editor sit up and pay attention!

After your manuscript has been typed and you've made your corrections, check it for spelling and punctuation errors. (Those of you who have a computer have a spell-check device that will catch many of your mistakes.) Even so, all of you should be interested in the list of "spelling demons" compiled by English teachers recently. For example, five of these words are misspelled. Can you find them?

abbreviate	wholely
garantee	marriageable
occurrence	dinosaur
truely	arguement
saccharin	idiosyncrasy
similar	development
harrassment	amateur
feasible	acquire
picnicking	grammar
competent	eccentric

The five misspelled words are *guarantee, truly, harassment, wholly* and *argument.*

If you are rather shaky about grammar, look through your *Elements of Style* by Strunk and White. Don't expect to be a topnotch grammarian overnight. If you are in a dither once in a while over a fine point, and can't find an answer anywhere, call a librarian to see if there is a "Dial-a-Grammarian" in your area. A number of colleges now feature them.

If you are a little uncertain about your punctuation, you can refer to the following pages. I have rounded up the punctuation issues that have plagued my students from time to time. First, let's take a look at quotation marks. Here are some basic rules.

1. Use quotations marks to enclose a direct quote.
   Example: Tom said, "The book is better than the movie."
2. Direct quotes, divided into two parts by an interrupting expression (he or she said), require quotation marks around both parts. The second part begins with a lowercase letter if it is part of the same sentence. If it is not, it begins with a capital.
   Example: "Why is it," my mother said, "that you always wait until the last minute to do your homework?"
   Example: "Be careful going down those stairs," Aunt Emma warned. "They are very rickety."
3. Commas and periods are always placed inside closing quotation marks.
   Example: The teacher read aloud "The Raven," a poem by Edgar Allan Poe.
4. Colons and semicolons are always placed outside the closing quotation marks.
   Example: The little girl cried, "It's mine"; the little boy ran away.
5. Use single quotation marks to enclose a quotation within a quotation.
   Example: "Didn't you hear me ask 'Where is the key?' " she inquired.

If you have forgotten some of the rules of capitalization, here are a few worth knowing.

1. Capitalize the first and important words in a title. It is not

necessary to capitalize *a*, *an* and *the*, or prepositions and conjunctions.

Example: "The Charge of the Light Brigade," Secretary of the Navy, Colonel James Potter

2. Capitalize sections of the country; they are not capitalized when they indicate direction.
   Example: I will be driving through the Midwest this summer.
   Example: Her house is south of town and difficult to find.

3. Do not capitalize the names of seasons unless personified.
   Example: I think spring is the best season of all.
   Example: Here is Spring in all her glory.

4. Do not capitalize words like *theater*, *hotel* and *high school* unless they are part of a proper name.
   Example: Yorktown High School, a high school student, Shoreham Hotel, a hotel in Washington

Finally, here are some of the other troublemakers to avoid in whipping up a good manuscript.

1. The number of the subject is not changed by a phrase following the subject.
   Example: One of the boys is coming to work today.
   Example: A knowledge of rules helps the student to use English correctly.

2. The following pronouns are singular: *each*, *either*, *neither*, *one*, *anyone*, *everybody*, *no one*, *nobody*, *anyone*, *someone* and *somebody*.
   Example: Neither girl has the right answer.

3. The following pronouns are plural: *few*, *several*, *many* and *both*.
   Example: Several of these plants are in need of water and special care.

4. The following pronouns may be either singular or plural: *all*, *some*, *most*, *any* and *none*.
   Example: Some of the cake was eaten. Some of the oranges were eaten.

   (*Some*, *most* and *all* are singular when they refer to a quantity of something, and plural when they refer to a number of things thought of individually.)

The following sentences contain some demons, too.
1. I can't walk one step farther. (Distance)
2. I will not discuss this any further. (Distance in abstract ideas)
3. This is strictly between you and me. (Between is a preposition and takes a direct object.)

Mailing It Out

When you are finally ready to mail out your brainchild, you can fold it into thirds if it's four pages or less, and enclose it in a #10 envelope. If you have five pages or more, place them in a folder and place it into a 10×13 envelope. Make sure you do not staple the pages; editors pass them around as they read them. Instead, Clip them together and make everybody happy.

If you are sending along illustrations or photographs, make sure that each piece has your name and address lightly penciled in on one corner of the back. Mark your envelope *Do Not Bend or Fold*. Clip your photo or artwork to the cardboard mentioned previously.

When you go to the post office with your precious cargo, you won't know ahead of time how much postage you will need to put on that return envelope, so don't seal the outer one until the clerk has weighed the entire package and you've affixed the necessary postage. You can mail it out First Class Mail or Special Fourth Class Rate: Manuscript. First class, of course, costs more, but your manuscript will get better handling and will travel faster. You should be aware that first class mail is forwarded and returned automatically; fourth class is not. To make sure you get your material back if it isn't delivered, print "Return Postage Guaranteed" under your return address.

Should you send a letter along with your submission? The experts advise against it. If, however, there is something you must explain, keep your letter brief and to the point. Don't suffer from the delusion that this bit of correspondence will make your submission look extra special to the editor. Whatever you are sending will always have to stand on its own merits. If you use fourth class mail, write "First Class Letter Enclosed" on the outside envelope, and pay the extra postage.

When you are mailing out a book manuscript, keep the pages loose and place them in a flat cardboard box with a cover; a typing paper box is ideal. Reinforce the corners of the box with tape so that it can't fall apart as it goes through the mails. Wrap it in brown mailing paper, and use labels for the addresses: Type them neatly so they are readable. It is wise to print the addresses directly on the package with a black pen in case the labels fall off en route to their destination. It is also a good idea to insure this important package of yours; if it should get lost, you'll have the funds ready for a new typing job. Let me reassure you about manuscripts disappearing: In my twenty years of writing, only one has gone to a distant planet.

If some of these details about sending out your manuscripts are confusing, here is a little summary.

1. A magazine needs: a one-page query letter
2. A nonfiction book needs: a query, an outline of each chapter and a sample chapter
3. A novel needs: a cover letter, a synopsis and three sample chapters

Editors have their own idiosyncratic pet peeves about manuscripts, but a number of them are in agreement on several that head their list. At the top is neglecting to send a self-addressed stamped envelope; the editor is under no obligation to return material that is not accompanied by that SASE. Another one is sending fiction to a nonfiction publication or the other way around. (You can avoid this by studying the magazine or newspaper you're aiming for, as I have suggested throughout this book.) Another is typing on transparent paper or using a dot-matrix printer. And finally, one that will be discussed further, sending out multiple submissions.

Multiple Submissions

It's one thing to send out a few query letters, but quite another to send out a few copies of an article, short story or book. It can be embarrassing to get two acceptances at the same time: Which one of the editors will you favor? What will you tell the rejected one? Even if you have never been put in this position before, friends of mine have been. They admit that it placed them in a quandary. What you can do is read carefully what the editors or publishers will accept.

Based on the research I've been doing lately, I can vouch for the fact that a number of book editors are accepting photocopied manuscripts and are going along with the idea of multiple submissions. But I think I can safely say that the majority of editors still expect to receive the original copy of your manuscript, and take it for granted that you have not sent the same version to anyone else. You'll soon see why many writers are becoming impatient with this setup: It's time-consuming to wait for months before you hear if you have made a sale. But for now it's the right thing to do.

How long should you wait before sending a note to the editor? The consensus seems to be about two months. If you haven't heard by then, type a short letter in which you ask politely about the status of your article, story or book. Make sure to send a SASE. Just one point: Realize that the editor has many other things to do, and also has to make judgments on other submissions.

Copyright

What about copyright? Suppose you have put the finishing touches to a 1,000-word article on a trip to the Bermuda Triangle. You have supplied gems of information that make this article very special. How can you protect it? All you have to do is request the proper form from the Copyright Office. Fill it out and send it, along with a $20 registration fee and one copy of your work (two if it's published), to: Register of Copyrights, Library of Congress, Washington, DC 20559.

You do not have to register each work individually. A group of articles can be registered at the same time if they meet the following requirements: They must be assembled in orderly fashion by placing them in a notebook binder; they must carry a single title ("Works by Sarah Jones," for example); they must represent the work of one person (or one set of collaborators); and they must be the subject of a single claim of copyright (you cannot claim an individual copyright for each article in the group; for copyright purposes, the group is now a single work). The entire group of articles, by the way, can be registered for $20.

If you want more information on copyright, write to the same address and ask for their free Copyright Information Kit. This office can answer specific questions, but does not give out legal advice.

As you go over these tips on how to prepare a manuscript, you are probably amazed by how much is involved. Even if you follow all of these suggestions to the letter, there is no guarantee that your work will be bought. But at least you will know that you are putting your best foot forward and making a good impression in the writing world. You're bound to come up a winner sooner or later!

 Assignment

You've decided to write that romance novel. Good, take a look at how to write a synopsis and write that first page. Now!

13 SENIOR SCRIBES

Time to retire? It's also the time to make one of your dreams come true: to become a writer. Through the years, you've always been fascinated by words. You scribbled them on the backs of envelopes or shopping lists or slips of paper, true? You've jotted down snatches of thought while traveling to New York or California or London. You've stashed away intriguing facts on all kinds of subjects in the ragbag of your mind. You knew that some day you'd be a writer. That day is here!

If you're hesitating, you're about to admit that you simply don't know how or where to begin. Should you try fiction first? Should you type up your travel notes into an article? Can a beginner break into print in one of the slick magazines? Is there a step-by-step process by which the novice can learn the craft of writing?

These were some of the questions the senior scribes asked in my classes on how to get started in writing. We met once a week for several years, and later became a kind of club; no one wanted the class to end. Now, twelve years later, we still meet once in a while to talk "shop" and to discuss new trends in the writing field. Many of these senior scribes have been published and will never forget the thrill of seeing their first bylines. They all started out by doing fillers, and then articles and, eventually, a short story.

What did they write about? Some were interested in nostalgia, others in holiday memories, and quite a few in American history.

Nostalgia

Here are some ideas if you choose nostalgia. What does that word actually mean? According to the dictionary, it is a desire to return in thought or fact to a former time in one's life, to one's home or to one's family and friends. It must, of course, be associated with emotion and bring back fond memories of long ago. Here are some questions that will take you back in time—and make you grab a pencil.

- What games did you play when you were a child? Can you remember "Statues" or "Kick the Can" or "Run, Sheep, Run"? Can you describe them?
- Who was your favorite teacher? Why? What was your favorite subject? Who was the worst-behaved boy (or girl) in the class? What became of him or her?
- How did you amuse yourself on a rainy day?
- Did you grow up in the Beatlemania era? What songs were your favorites? What did teenagers do for fun during that time frame?
- Are you a product of the Roaring Twenties? Can you remember saying "Oh, you kid!" or dancing the Charleston or singing "Bye, Bye, Blackbird" or "When Day Is Done"? Those were the days when a woman in the family was practically condemned to death if she bobbed her hair. Did it happen to you or someone in your family?

Probably one of the easiest ways to reminisce is to think about Christmases past. Walter Olesky, who writes for *Modern Maturity* magazine, interviewed a number of celebrities in 1979 and asked them to think about a Christmas they would never forget. They responded with a variety of answers; here are some excerpts.

Lillian Gish: When I was five years old and touring on the road with a melodrama, Christmas found our company in Detroit. . . . One of the cast members asked me what I wanted Santa to bring me, and I replied, "A comb, a mirror and a muff."

Christmas fell on Saturday, and between the matinee and the evening performances, some men came backstage and asked to take me across the alley to an automobile agency. In the center of their showroom was an enormous Christmas tree, and under it, three brightly wrapped packages.

When I opened them, I found a comb, a mirror and a muff.

James Roosevelt: My favorite Christmas was the first time I was allowed to join the family and hear my father read "A Christmas Carol." He not only read it to his children . . . but later to his grandchildren.

Lawrence Welk: All my Christmases were memorable! I can still remember vividly how my seven brothers and sisters and I would wait with anguished anticipation for the arrival of St. Nicholas on the night before Christmas. All eight of us would perch rigidly on the edge of our chairs in the kitchen, waiting anxiously for the sound of sleigh bells outside.

The moment we heard the sleigh bells, Father would fling open the door—and there he'd be, St. Nicholas himself, all rosy and red, garbed in a scarlet suit, with white whiskers flowing down over his ample chest, a big smile on his face, a twinkle in his eye and a dreaded question on his lips:

"Have you boys and girls been good little boys and girls this year?"

George Burns: Doesn't it seem strange to be asking Jewish people about the Christmas they'll never forget? I came from a very poor and very large family. My family was raised Orthodox, so Christmas was not our holiday, but Hanukkah was almost the equivalent. The Hanukkah I'll never forget is the one when for a present I got one roller skate. That's right, just one skate. I think it fit either foot, and where it came from I don't know. Come to think of it, I never did get the other one.

(*Modern Maturity*, 1979–1980)

Is there a Christmas that really stands out in your mind? Or a special Thanksgiving? Accounts of these two holidays must be different and outstanding to impress the editor of a newspaper or magazine. You may have more luck getting an acceptance by trying to remember a Fourth of July or a terrifying Halloween from the past. But I did come across a Christmas story recently with a touch of whimsy about it that made it delightful to read. A freelancer by the name of Floyce Larson told about the Christmas when her Norwegian grandmother visited her Wisconsin farm and related the old legend about animals speaking on Christmas morning. As the two of them baked bread for the animals on the farm, Floyce was tempted to mention the fact that she had tried on her mother's gold ring, and that it had somehow come off her finger. She searched all over and couldn't find it anywhere. We pick up her story on Christmas Eve.

After church, we all stayed up later than usual. We sat around the kitchen table drinking hot chocolate and eating popcorn while sister made fudge on the old wood cooking stove.

It was almost midnight when I finally lit the kerosene lantern and headed for the barn with my basket. I had loaves of rye, pumpernickel and whole wheat, corn muffins and even some raised potato donuts.

The sleeping animals came alive when they heard me. I tore off chunks of dark rye for the cows, and gave portions to the pigs, who grunted their approval. Lambs nuzzled my basket, and each received a corn muffin. . . .

For Prince, the horse, I saved a special loaf of whole wheat. . . . Something about him caught my attention. Staring at me in a strange manner, he opened his mouth. I would have sworn on my Confirmation Bible that I heard him say:

"Seek again."

Something compelled me to hang the lantern on a hook as I looked at the pile of hay. There, glinting like a star, was the precious gold ring. . . . So far as I know, Prince never spoke again.

I left home a few years after that special, magical night. But whenever I returned while Prince was still alive, I went out to the barn to pay him a visit. As I patted him on the nose and offered him a little treat, it seemed he gave me a knowing nod. And always, some mystical feeling passed between us.

(*Washington Post*, December 24, 1980)

The Historical Angle

If you are a history buff, your nostalgia articles or fillers can take a different turn, and give the readers a fascinating account of what it was like to live many years ago. For example, one of my students wrote up a kind of "You Are There" article on fourth graders visiting the home of Robert E. Lee in Arlington. She was especially interested in the project because her daughter was one of the students. Shelby Lawrence described what it was like to live in a white-pillared mansion in Virginia more than 150 years ago. She then told about children being received on the mansion's commanding portico by a gracious hoop-skirted lady and going on a tour of the house. After learning some facts about the Lee family, the students were divided into four groups. A short time later . . .

> A heavenly smell soon drifts from the kitchen where the young cooks are baking battercakes, which they will devour with honey. In the greenhouse, hands start cuttings and bulbs on a new life. At the same time, a kindly gentleman in woolen workclothes prowls the grounds, the cellar and the attic with his group, noting how native materials were transformed into the handsome neo-Grecian dwelling. In the attic, the fourth group of students digs into trunks filled with waves of taffeta and crinoline. Before long, several twentieth-century girls are transformed into giggling Southern belles. There on a table, crocks hold herbs and spices to be ground for sachets.
>
> (*Arlington News*, June 14, 1972)

Shelby ended her short feature by saying that when this trip into the past was finished, each student was reluctant to board the bus and return to the present. The members of my writing class enjoyed her story, and she had it published in a local paper.

Repasts of the Past

The kitchen of long ago seems to be a focal point for many nostalgia pieces these days, and one that I found appealing was written by Goody Solomon, a columnist for the *Fairfax Journal*. She described her mother's 1930s kitchen in New York City where she grew up, and told about coming home from school and finding her mother chopping chicken livers, koshering meats or scrubbing and polishing. She also recalled how important it was to have fresh vegetables every day in her household and to have balanced and nutritious meals. She emphasized that her mother didn't even own a cookbook, but managed to turn out appetizing food. The lengthy column also revealed that prepackaged items were frowned upon, and *good* meant fresh foods, carefully chosen and prepared. Goody's mother believed in steaming string beans, baking or boiling potatoes, and broiling meats and fish. Goody's own interest in food and nutrition probably stems from those early days.

Did you ever go to a general store when you were growing up? How about taking us there and sharing with us some of the atmosphere and the goodies you found? If your memory needs a bit of jogging, here are some things that will help you go back in time: wooden counters and cases; a vintage cash register; a potbelly stove; a working post office that hand-cancels mail with its own stamp; shelves crowded with baskets; craft books; brooms; stuffed calico cats; posters; and dolls. And don't forget those glass jugs chock-full of penny candy: jawbreakers, fruit slices and licorice twists. Add your own little remembrances and write up an article that will make us wistful for that special store.

Food also plays an important role in thinking about the past. Mimi Sheraton wrote an article on memories of hot cereal mornings that without a doubt made many readers recall winter mornings when they were children and fervently wished they could stay under the covers instead of getting up for school. What really helped in facing the morning was the thought of a bowl of steaming hot cereal and cream. The author whets our appetite with

> If the rest of the world presented a foreboding frost-white picture, the kitchen at least was a fragrant, steaming center of warmth and well-being.
>
> Coffee was perking for grownups, perhaps cocoa was simmering for children, cinnamon toast might be gilding under the broiler, and the sharp, tropical scent of freshly sliced oranges added a reminder of summer. A peek into the bubbling pot told us which cereal was on the daily menu and, if memory

serves correctly, my mother kept a regular store of a dozen or so varieties.

.... As much as I loved the creamy cereals the day they were cooked, I adored them even more the second day, when leftover "mush" was cut into squares and slowly fried in butter until both sides were golden brown.

(New York Times Company, 1978)

This article ran about 1,000 words and followed all the rules of good writing. Sheraton used specifics whenever possible so that we could smell and see and taste those breakfasts. And whenever she did use an adjective, she made it count. Some of her verbs also added special effects: *perking . . . simmering . . .* gilding.

What about markets? Check with your local newspaper. Some of them are interested in hearing from retirees. But look up the markets in *Writer's Market.* You'll find editors interested not only in nostalgia, history and memories of long ago, but in your travel tips and descriptions of the places you visited. If you know how to invest, write about it. Share your tips on dieting and how you won the battle with cholesterol.

Once upon a time, there were only three or four markets out there for seniors. Now there are thirteen! Read them over and send a filler or an article. You will get a byline and some money—a great combination.

 Assignment

Write about the day you retired and how you felt at the time. One of my senior scribes came up with a quip, "I'm working on my senility. Everyday I make it a point to forget at least one thing." Did you take it all in stride? Were there any funny moments?

EPILOGUE

There are two important words to add now to your vocabulary: *discipline* and *perseverance*. There will be times when the Muse will not come and perch on your shoulder, and inspiration will have to come from you. Make yourself sit there and make those creative juices flow. Ignore the crazy excuses you'll have: It's too hot to write; it's too cold to write; the furnace is making a funny noise; I have to answer that letter from Uncle Fred; I can't work on my novel until I decide whether to name the heroine Jennie or Jasmine, and so on. You'll be making excuses of your own before long. Wait and see.

The second word, *perseverance*, means to keep at it no matter what. You have read about some of the rejection slips sent to famous writers, but that fact won't help when you open that envelope and find yours. Look your work over and then send it out again— and again. In the meantime, get started on another filler or article or short story. Don't ever have only one item making the rounds. But guess what? The day will come when you will find an acceptance note in that envelope.

The chapters in this book have told you many things: How to write fillers, articles, short stories and novels. They have given you all kinds of ideas for writing a column. They have supplied the necessary details of how to make your manuscript look professional. They have given you good advice on finding markets. But something is missing.

Nowhere have you been told how thrilling it is to see your first byline. Nowhere have you been told that eventually your words will make your readers laugh or cry, or send a shiver up and down their spine. Your words! Your teenager would call that "awesome." And it is.

The day will come when you will be right up there with a number of those famous authors, past and present. Don't forget the fact that they, too, were unknowns once upon a time. If they could do it, so can you. Begin today!

INDEX